THE RISE AND FALL OF THE ROYAL SHAKESPEARE COMPANY

Also by Simon Trowbridge

NON-FICTION

The Music of Bruce Springsteen
and the E Street Band

The Comédie-Française from
Molière to Éric Ruf

Rameau

The Company

FICTION

Élodie Duquette

The Rise *and* Fall *of the* Royal Shakespeare Company

An Illustrated History

SIMON TROWBRIDGE

ENGLANCE *PRESS*

First published by
Englance Press, Oxford, in 2021

Paperback Edition, 2022

Copyright © 2021, 2022 by Simon Trowbridge

All rights reserved. No part of this book may be reproduced, copied, adapted, displayed, stored, distributed or transmitted in any form.

ISBN 978-1-7392053-1-7

Frontispiece:
Peter Brook, Michel Saint-Denis and Peter Hall photographed at the RSC in Stratford in March 1963. Photograph by the *Daily Express* / Hulton Archive, Getty Images.

To Dinah

King Lear by Shakespeare, 1964. Production: Peter Brook. Photograph by Angus McBean / ullstein bild via Getty Images.

Contents

Preface		11
PART ONE		
1 Beginnings		17
1	Charles Flower	19
2	William Bridges-Adams	24
2 The Post-War Years		31
1	Barry Jackson	33
2	The Glamorous 1950s	40
PART TWO		
3 Peter Hall		49
1	The Road to Stratford	52
2	Making the RSC	56
3	The Question of Subsidy	71
4	Michel Saint-Denis	78
5	Peter Brook	83
6	Defeating the Censor	91
7	John Barton	92
8	Handing Over	95
9	Peter Hall's RSC: Some Representative Actors	96
4 Trevor Nunn and Terry Hands		105
1	Transition	108
2	National Theatres	114
3	The Importance of Small-scale Work	121

4	Nunn's Style	128
5	Terry Hands and the Main Stage	134
6	The Swan	138
7	The End of the Nunn/Hands Era	142
8	Nunn/Hands's RSC: Some Representative Actors	150

5 Adrian Noble — 163
1	Background	166
2	The 1990s	170
3	Innovation and Controversy	177
4	Noble's RSC: Some Representative Actors	182

PART THREE

6 A New Era — 191
1	Semtex Boyd	193
2	Building a New Theatre	197
3	One Company or Many?	201
4	Gregory Doran	208
5	The Future: Think Big	210

Notes — 212

Index — 220

Preface

When I started to write about the Royal Shakespeare Company, in the 1980s, I was motivated by my enthusiasm for what was then considered to be one of Britain's most important cultural achievements since the war – the creation of the country's first national theatre troupe. However, in around 2000, the leaders of the RSC began to jettison most of the key principles established by the company's founder Peter Hall, and in 2002 they gave up the Company's London home. Today, as Terry Hands recently told me,[1] the RSC is a brand name, and no longer a company.

When people at the top of the RSC first started to declare that Peter Hall's model of a permanent company of actors performing both classical and modern works in repertory was no longer sustainable, I gave them the benefit of the doubt. But then I spent several years writing a book about France's national theatre company, the Comédie-Française. By performing whole seasons of work in London in 1871 and 1879, the Comédie-Française provoked in many of the people who saw them a longing for the establishment of an English national theatre company capable of serving the language and ideas of Shakespeare as the Comédiens-Français served the language and ideas of Molière. Matthew Arnold was the most prominent of the influential figures who published essays and letters on this theme. Arnold's *The French Play in London*, published in the journal *Nineteenth Century*, was nothing less than a manifesto for a reformed theatre. His words would be taken up by younger men such as Bernard Shaw and Harley Granville-Barker and the struggle would begin to make their dreams real. The

RSC and the National Theatre were finally established at the beginning of the 1960s.

Here, for me, is the point. Over three hundred years since the Comédie-Française was founded by Louis XIV, this troupe remains true to its founding principles. It is sometimes assumed that, because of its rules and long history, the Comédie-Française must be moribund, but I found this not to be true. There have been good and less good periods of work, of course, and there are some disadvantages as well as advantages in the troupe's system of governance, but, overall, people in France recognise the artistic and wider cultural value of the existence of at least one permanent troupe, motivated by excellence, shared values and a mission to constantly renew the great works of French dramatic literature, not least by placing them in a continuous dialogue with foreign masterpieces and new works.

In creating the RSC, Hall adopted a number of the key principles that underpin the Comédie-Française, and his successors Trevor Nunn and Terry Hands (who was a director at the Comédie-Française) believed in them passionately too. While it is true that Hall and Nunn never wanted the RSC to be bound by the rigid rules that lock down the actors of the Comédie-Française, wanting instead to build into the structure a flexibility that would allow RSC actors the freedom to take breaks from the Company to appear on the screen, they did want a nucleus of players (named *associates*) to make a true commitment over many years, and to play a number of different kinds of role, in repertory, during the seasons (the system of *alternance* as defined by the Comédie). And, while, unlike the *sociétaires* of the Comédie, the associates were not given significant power, Hall wanted this nucleus of players to create a collective style of playing that would be recognisably RSC. The securing of a London home was essential, for no actor could be expected to work exclusively at Stratford year after year. All this was achieved. Hall also wanted the RSC to be a company of directors, designers and other artists. This was a crucial part of his vision. It was essential that the actors worked regularly with directors who had invested in the Company and believed in its methods and style. His team included Peter Brook, Michel Saint-Denis, John Barton, Clifford Williams, David Jones, Trevor Nunn and Terry Hands.

Nunn and Hands, during the 1970s and 80s, added the younger members Adrian Noble, Howard Davies, Barry Kyle, Ron Daniels and Bill Alexander. These artists directed by far the majority of RSC productions during the period, as well as taking on management roles and contributing to policy-making.

The company system began to loosen at the end of the 1990s and was essentially abandoned by 2015. Methods and goals should be challenged, re-thought, modified and even abandoned: a theatre shouldn't be a museum. The RSC under Nunn was not the same as the RSC under Hall. The Comédie-Française of today is not an exact copy of the Comédie-Française of the 19th century. Principles, though, are worth preserving. I'm aware that the views expressed in this preface are idealistic, and that the notion of even a semi-permanent company within the market-orientated English theatre has always been problematic – to create and preserve a company requires considerable will and talent. But the rewards are worth fighting for.

This book, therefore, has become unashamedly polemical. It proclaims the special significance of the principles established by Hall and nurtured by Nunn and Hands. It challenges the view that states that because today's leading actors won't sign long contracts Hall's ideas are no longer achievable in England. The RSC should be making stars (as it did in its heyday), not chasing them. The leading players of the Comédie-Française are stars because they are members of the Comédie-Française. This book declares that our theatre was richer when the RSC adhered to the ensemble principle and the repertory system. For as things stand, Arnold needs to re-write his essay and Shaw and Granville-Barker need to re-start the work of creating a national theatre troupe in England.

This book is dedicated to my sister in memory of our parents, Bill and Rita Trowbridge. My mother wasn't a great theatre-goer, but at the age of eighteen, in 1948, she saw Paul Scofield in *The Winter's Tale* at Stratford and kept the programme he signed for her. When my father was a young merchant seaman, he would spend his short periods of leave in London attending West End shows. We saw many productions together during his later years and would talk about them on the long drive home. I particularly remember his pleasure at seeing *Hamlet* at the Barbican in 1989, and *Troilus and Cressida*, *Cymbeline*, *Pericles*, T.S. Eliot's *The Family Reunion* and David Pownall's *Elgar's Rondo* at Stratford during the 1990s. He especially admired Peter Hall's productions of the plays of Shaw at Bath and Marianne Elliott's *Saint Joan* at the National. Going to the theatre was very consoling for him after my mother died.

My thanks go to the photographers of the powerful images reproduced in this book, especially Donald Cooper.

PART ONE

The Shakespeare Memorial Theatre, Stratford. Above: ca.1895. Below: 1932.

1
Beginnings

Hamlet by Shakespeare, SMT, 1936. Valerie Tudor (Ophelia), Donald Wolfit (Hamlet). Production: Iden Payne. Photograph by Lebrecht Music and Arts / Alamy.

1   Charles Flower

The story begins in 1875 when a Victorian beer maker called Charles Edward Flower founded the Shakespeare Memorial Theatre in Stratford. Peter Hall transformed and remodelled the organisation in 1961, changing its name to the Royal Shakespeare Theatre (RST), but we must give Charles Flower his due.

Charles's father established the Flower brewery business in Stratford in 1832. It delivered great wealth and inculcated a deep sense of civic responsibility. Charles, who took over the management of the brewery on his father's retirement, was both mayor and magistrate. He was typical of his class and his age, the kind of Victorian too easily parodied today. This is how he was described after his death:

> Mr Flower was not only generous but genial, courteous but kindly, firm but faithful, full of humour, familiar with books, a good talker and willing listener, a man of much travel, and therefore of broad views; an excellent host, without form or ceremony; a clear-sighted, manly Englishman, whose name and memory will always be honoured by all who knew him well, and whose good and generous works and gifts will ever be remembered in the pleasant places to which Shakespeare has given undying fame.[2]

Charles Flower was among those dignitaries who felt that the town had not done enough to honour its famous son. The only significant commemoration of the poet, the Jubilee of 1769 organised by David Garrick, was remembered for all the wrong reasons.

The great actor's performances at the Theatre Royal, Drury Lane, in versions of Shakespeare's plays designed to appeal to contemporary taste, were instrumental in helping to make the poet a figure of national reverence. Garrick attempted to persuade the rich and connected of London society to gather out of town for a three-day festival by promising a masquerade ball, the performance of an ode to Shakespeare, with music by Thomas Arne, and a spectacular pageant. The venue was a flimsily built wooden pavilion erected beside the Avon. As if to mock Garrick and Arne's sentimental song 'Soft Flowing Avon', just premiered, heavy rain caused the river to spill its banks and the site was flooded. Some of the events, including the pageant, had to be cancelled. Garrick lost a small fortune.

As the leading organiser of the events marking the tercentenary of Shakespeare's birth in 1864, Charles Flower decided to place performances of several of Shakespeare's plays, in a temporary playhouse, at the centre of the celebrations. Many people in the town would have preferred a memorial in the form of a statue, while the London press dismissed the idea as over-ambitious. Indeed, the performances, by the company of the Princess's Theatre, London, made a considerable loss, which the Flowers covered out of their own pockets. For Charles Flower, though, the idea of building a permanent theatre in Stratford as a memorial to Shakespeare grew into an obsession and, despite the failure of 1864, he pursued its realisation stubbornly.

Flower was not only a man who got things done. He had serious ideas about the stage and wanted his theatre to be revolutionary. The English stage of the 19th century was ruled by privately-owned commercial enterprises. There was no public (or, for that matter, private) funding, no government involvement (beyond censorship), no genuine ensembles, no organisation, few new plays of merit and no unabridged productions of the plays of Shakespeare. The best England had to offer was the work of a few famous actors who leased theatres and engaged players to support their own performances. Henry Irving at the Lyceum was the most eminent actor-manager of the 1870s and 80s. This chaotic state of affairs had been tolerated for generations despite the richness of England's theatrical heritage.

Flower's foundation of a theatre in Stratford coincided with the beginning of a movement that called out England's disregard for its theatre culture and which sought to affect change. The catalyst was the arrival in London of France's Comédie-Française. France's renowned national troupe performed entire seasons of work in the capital in 1871 and 1879. The first visit was motivated by the Comédie's need to raise funds at a time of political turmoil. Their theatre needed substantial repairs, and they couldn't operate fully in Paris because of the rules inflicted on them by the Commune. Around half of the company travelled to London and, between 2 May and 8 June, performed over thirty plays in repertory at the Opera Comique (off the Strand). The troupe was feted by politicians, artists and the London press. Eight years later, the entire troupe took up a residency at the Gaiety Theatre. The presence of Sarah Bernhardt and other star actors turned the season into something of a media circus, but the lesson of the Comédie's two seasons was clear: a permanent company brings style, excellence and the means of truly ensuring that the great classics are realised truthfully (i.e. not as star vehicles) while also providing an impetus for new writing. The Comédie performed controversial new plays by Dumas *fils* as well as masterpieces by Molière, Racine and Corneille. Of the commentators and artists who attended the performances and longed for an English national company, the most prominent was Matthew Arnold, who wrote an essay on this theme in the journal *Nineteenth Century*:

> What are we to learn then from the marvellous success and attractiveness of the performances at the Gaiety Theatre? […] Surely it is this: 'The theatre is irresistible; organise the theatre.' […] The performances of the French company show us plainly, I think, what is gained […] by organising the theatre. An older drama, containing many things of high merit, some things of surpassing merit, is kept before the public by means of this company, is given frequently, is given to perfection. Pieces of truth and beauty, which emerge here and there among the questionable pieces of the modern drama, get the benefit of this company's skill, and are given to perfection. […] The organisation in the example before us is simple and rational. We have a society of good actors, with a grant from the State on condition of their giving with frequency the classic stage-plays of their

nation, and with a commissioner of the State attached to the society and taking part in the council with it. But the society is to all intents and purpose self-governing. In connexion with it is the school of dramatic elocution of the Conservatoire. [The Comédie-Française has] traditions, effect, consistency, and a place in the public esteem. [...] We have in England everything to make us dissatisfied with the chaotic and ineffective condition into which our theatre has fallen. We have the remembrance of better things in the past, and the elements for better things in the future. We have a splendid national drama of the Elizabethan age, and a later drama which has no lack of pieces conspicuous by their stage-qualities, their vivacity and their talent. We have had great actors. We have good actors not a few at the present moment. But we have been unlucky, as we so often are, in the work of organisation. In the essay at organisation which we had, in the patent theatres with their exclusive privilege of acting Shakespeare, we find by no means an example, such as we have in the constitution of the French Theatre, of what a judicious man, seeking that good of the drama and of the public, would naturally devise.[3]

It was from this beginning that the movement to establish a national theatre troupe in England would grow. It is unknown whether Charles Flower saw the Comédie in London, but he would have read the many editorials and reviews in *The Times* provoked by the two seasons, and was surely thinking of the Comédie, as well as the privately-funded Meiningen Company, the European example he cited, when he told the assembled guests at the Mayor's banquet in Stratford in November 1876:

The actors feel an *esprit de corps*, and work together as members of one body. In every representation the whole of the company is employed, and the actor who takes a leading role one evening may take a minor one the next. [...] The result is a production as near perfection as possible, and the prestige of the company is great.[4]

Flower, as a businessman, may not have believed that a theatre should be funded by the state, but he did believe that it should be released from the shackles of commerce by means of private funding. We find in his speech the aspiration to create a genuine company, and it is revealing that his comments pre-echo Matthew Arnold's of just a few years later. While the journey would be long and tortuous, Flower was setting out on an adventure that would eventually reach the destination that both he and Arnold longed for.

In 1875, Flower convened a body called the Council for the Shakespeare Memorial Association to achieve the construction of a theatre, library and art gallery. Registered under the Companies Act, the Council started the process of raising funds from public subscriptions. Flower persevered despite the incredulity of the London papers. He donated a considerable stretch of land beside the Avon from Clopton Bridge to Holy Trinity Church, the cottages across the road, and most of the funding. Dodgshun and Unsworth's design of a semi-circular redbrick building with medieval and Tudor features, including turrets and a tower, was constructed between 1877 and 1879; the area around it was landscaped into gardens. The horseshoe-shaped interior had a circle and a gallery, and a conventional proscenium stage. The members of the Council for the Shakespeare Memorial Association became the theatre's governors, and performances were entrusted to visiting companies (the festival lasted for eight days each spring).

Charles Flower was a pioneer, but the London press saw a presumptuous provincial dreamer. Those who wanted an English national theatre were dismissive of the notion that it could be created in a small market town and not in London. The fact that Flower's theatre was built surprised the sceptics and led some to soften their attitudes, but others remained derisive, viewing Flower's project as an act of hubris. Who, among the gentry of Warwickshire, *The Daily Telegraph* asked, would want to watch a play by Shakespeare? The question was not unreasonable. For many decades, Stratford would have to rely on local audiences, and the demand wasn't there to extend the festival or to allow Flower's vision of a permanent company to be realised. Instead, Stratford had to be content with employing actor-managers who had lost their lustre in London and who brought with them their own band of second and third-rate actors. The company of the Irish tragedian Barry Sullivan, nearly fifty and way beyond his glory days, inaugurated the theatre in April 1879 with performances of *Much Ado About Nothing*, *Hamlet* and *As You Like It*. Hamlet was Sullivan's most famous role. For the first and only time before 1932, the London papers sent their theatre critics to Stratford. The critical notices were predictably scathing but not unfair.

In 1886, Frank Benson[5] began thirty-three years of bringing his company to the festival. After seven frustrating years, the engagement of Benson must have filled Flower with hope. Benson was a new man. He was only in his twenties and he was more in the mould of Irving than of Sullivan. He professed to believe in the company ethos so valued by Flower, but this was window-dressing. Once established, Benson didn't play a single minor role, and as he aged he gradually went the same way as Sullivan. The same productions were repeated year after year and Benson remained wedded to Victorian prudery all his life. The fact that Benson and his actors were loved by Stratford audiences helped to prolong his regime long after it had become moribund. Benson delivered continuity but little in the way of innovation or excitement.

2 William Bridges-Adams

Charles Flower died suddenly in 1892 and was succeeded as chairman by his brother Edgar, who kept the theatre going without becoming personally engaged in the work; he was succeeded in 1903 by his son Archibald, who shared Charles's passion. After the Great War, Archibald Flower finally broke with the ageing and debt-ridden Benson and secured, in 1919, the SMT's first resident company and first managing director, William Bridges-Adams.[6]

It was a crucial step forward. The company was initially part-funded and co-governed by the committee seeking the establishment of a National Theatre in London. Since a National Theatre building remained a far-off prospect, its advocates, including Bernard Shaw and Harley Granville-Barker, were willing to support Bridges-Adams's new company, although they never intended to elevate the SMT or include it in their long-term plans.[7] Funding was withdrawn after a few years. Shaw's support, though, was genuine – he became a Stratford governor – and lasting.

Bridges-Adams was a director in the modern sense. Younger than Granville-Barker, he was inspired by his intellectual approach; but he also valued spectacle and the romance of the Victorian stage. He wanted to produce the plays uncut and he wanted a permanent company. Realising his vision for Stratford proved to be almost impossible. There were now two short seasons, the first in the spring, the second in the summer. He lengthened both, but was unable to establish adequate rehearsal periods, meaning that he worked under constant pressure and was forced to cut the texts after all. If the quality of the acting was mixed, there were some fine players. From 1925, Bridges-Adams built many of his seasons around the veteran Randle Ayrton, a distinguished Shakespearean who seemed indifferent to the London stage and its rewards. Younger actors admired by Bridges-Adams included Sebastian Shaw, who played Romeo, Ferdinand in *The Tempest* and Prince Hal to Ayrton's Falstaff in the two parts of *Henry IV* in 1926, and John Laurie, who played Hamlet in 1927. There was never enough money. The motor car was bringing visitors to Stratford but it would take time for the theatre to see the benefits at the box office.

Bridges-Adams was hampered by the inadequacies of the Shakespeare Memorial Theatre. The building was picturesque but small. Shaw shared Bridges-Adams's frustration. Speaking at the luncheon to celebrate Shakespeare's birthday in 1925, he called for a new theatre. Less than a year later, on the afternoon of 7 March 1926, a fire broke out at the back of the stage that reduced the auditorium to a blackened shell within hours (the picture gallery and library survived). The cause of the fire was not discovered. The building was closed and empty of people at the time, but theatre staff had been inside during the morning.[8] A carelessly thrown cigarette was the suspected cause. Shaw responded to the news of the blaze by sending Archibald Flower a telegram: 'Congratulations. It will be a tremendous advantage to have a proper modern building. There are a number of other theatres I should like to see burned down.'[9]

Archibald Flower converted the Stratford Picture House (yet another Flower-owned property) into a temporary theatre, and launched an appeal to raise the £250,000 needed to build a new

SMT. He had wanted a new theatre before the fire; the safe option of restoring the original was never considered. In seeking support for the campaign, he wrote: 'May I give the assurance that the Governors of the Stratford-upon-Avon Memorial Theatre wish to get the best architectural advice which the world can give. There is at present a crying need for a theatre which will give to the world performances of Shakespeare comparable with the Wagner performances at Bayreuth. Is there a more fitting place for such a theatre than the town which gave England's greatest poet to the world?'[10] The appeal was supported by the party leaders – Stanley Baldwin, Ramsay MacDonald and H.H. Asquith – and by artists of the calibre of Shaw, who donated one hundred guineas, and Thomas Hardy, but it proved impossible to raise such a large sum to build a theatre in Britain during the depression of the late 1920s and early 1930s. Flower turned successfully to the financial great of America: John D. Rockefeller alone gave £100,000. The success of the campaign provoked a revealingly negative response from the London cultural elite. Granville-Barker was so anxious on behalf of the national theatre movement that he wrote a letter to *The Times* on the matter:

> An extravagant expenditure on building, machinery and endowment will not be of real benefit to Stratford. There is such a thing as having too much money, if you cannot profitably employ it. Further, there is the question of the Shakespeare National Theatre, which many of us hope to see set up some day in London. If Stratford is to absorb over a quarter of a million and still be hungry for more, the critics of the larger National Theatre Scheme may assume that London's need will be for a million or so, and relegate it on these grounds still further into the realm of impracticabilities.[11]

Over seventy architects from Britain and America entered the design competition: the winning entry, chosen by the Royal Institute of Architects, was a modernist design, relatively simple and functional, by the inexperienced Elizabeth Scott, a junior member of a minor London firm. The great-niece of Sir George Gilbert Scott, she was the first woman to design a major building in

England. Archibald Flower and Bridges-Adams sought a world-class theatre with the most up-to-date stage machinery and lighting, fine sightlines and a sense of intimacy. They accompanied Elizabeth Scott on a tour of French and German theatres, and took advice from Barry Jackson and Theodore Komisarjevsky, among others. Even today, many would share Bridges-Adams's aspirations for the new theatre: 'There is the need for absolute flexibility, a box of tricks out of which the child-like mind of the producer may create whatever shape it pleases.'[12] Unfortunately, the Royal Institute chose a design that ignored most of Bridges-Adams's initial specifications. The director was frustrated by the board's refusal to back him. He knew that fundamental mistakes had been made: the proscenium was too small for the size of the stage, the distance between the proscenium and the front of the stalls was too wide (the forestage could not be used in conjunction with the rolling stages), the circle was too far back, sightlines were inadequate from some sections of the auditorium, and the backstage was rudimentary with too few dressing-rooms and no green room.

Nevertheless, the new building confirmed the growing importance of Stratford. The London newspapers no longer mocked and the national theatre movement had stagnated. In previewing the new theatre, *The Guardian* wrote:

> The completion of this great enterprise – a substitute for the National Theatre which shows no sign of materialising – is an event of world interest and Stratford is hoping the world will send its representatives to witness the trial flight of the Swan of Avon in his fresh theatrical plumage. A fierce battle has been raging over the design. When one catches sight of it – as one comes into the town by the Clopton Bridge – the effect is startling. At the river's edge rises an enormous block of red brick topped by a monstrous square tower which seems to bestride the picturesque roofs and timbered houses of Shakespeare's town like a brutal modern Colossus. At first sight Miss Elisabeth Scott's creation seems in violent disharmony with the Stratford picture. On the other hand, the simple mass makes a peculiar impression of power. The theatre looks like what it is - the expression in modern monumental terms of homage to greatness.[13]

The building was quickly nicknamed the 'jam factory'. People also compared it to a gaol and a power station. *The Guardian* reported that Edward Elgar, a former Stratford resident who had loved the original theatre and whose symphonic study *Falstaff* (1913) was one of the great responses to a Shakespeare text in music, would conduct the orchestra during the opening season, and it is true that the great man had been approached by Flower. However, he changed his mind on the spot when Flower gave him a tour of the building. 'It is so unspeakably wrong,' he said. Flower and Bridges-Adams's had to work hard to dissuade him from writing to *The Times* on the matter.[14] The view of *The Times* was particularly important and, thankfully, its editor wanted to be positive. *The Times* declared that Stratford now had the 'best equipped theatre of the day' and reported: 'Most of [the opening day] visitors appeared to be of the opinion that the building was more impressive, even more friendly, than photographs had led them to expect'.[15]

The Royal opening on 23 April 1932, consisting of speeches and the performance of both parts of Shakespeare's *Henry IV*, was a major event that had more to do with civic and national pride than with the contemporary stage. The Prince of Wales declared that 'Shakespeare was above all things an Englishman',[16] and departed during the first interval. The spring season was not a critical success. The London critics only reviewed the first part of *Henry IV*, and under the intense pressure of the gala opening the actors didn't perform well and expectations were not met. The highlight of the season was a new staging by Bridges-Adams of *A Midsummer Night's Dream*, designed by Norman Wilkinson. While gauzes were used to conjure the nocturnal forest, the production's modernity was apparent in its deliberate juxtapositions – Puck wore a red hunting jacket.

The royal stamp of approval meant everything to Archibald Flower. His belief that the prestige of the opening had been wrecked by a poor performance seemed to change his thinking in a profound way. Bridges-Adams was equally frustrated, and disputes between the two men – over the size of the budget and over the quality of the acting (the view of Bridges-Adams's detractors was that he placed design above good performances) – came to a head.

Bridges-Adams insisted on remaining faithful to his company, the actors who had worked at Stratford during the last few years, but Flower wanted to engage bigger names. Bridges-Adams wanted to exploit the size of the new stage and the machinery; Flower wanted traditional productions. Bridges-Adams was showing an almost Peter Hall-like ambition, fighting the board to bring in Komisarjevsky and Tyrone Guthrie, replacing painted cloths with three-dimensional settings, and negotiating with the Old Vic to bring Stratford shows to London. Thanks to the successful funding campaigns and prudent investments, the SMT had become a relatively wealthy theatre. The new building with its large auditorium had opened just as the town was filling with visitors, meaning that the seasons going forward should make a profit. Bridges-Adams wanted to access the reserves to 'think big'.

Komisarjevsky was the most innovative producer of the time, a director-designer who interpreted Shakespeare through questioning foreign eyes. It was a coup to bring him to Stratford, and his production of *The Merchant of Venice* during the 1932 summer season, daring and deliberately divisive, but successful at the box office, should have vindicated Bridges-Adams's policies, but Flower had already decided to dismiss him at the end of his current contract. Bridges-Adams wasn't told but could see where things were going. 1933 saw the introduction of a major innovation, the creation of a single season lasting from April to September (Flower reluctantly agreed). The impressive programme included the return of Komisarjevsky to direct *Macbeth*, a staging that showcased his expressionism – shadows loomed against the aluminium walls of the set. Alongside Macbeth, Guthrie staged *Richard II* and Bridges-Adams directed the young Rachel Kempson in *Romeo and Juliet*. The season, Bridges-Adams's last as managing director, was a commercial success. While his policies were too innovative for the conservative elderly man Flower had become, there was also the issue of their personal relationship – it was beyond repair. In April 1934, Bridges-Adams resigned to avoid the humiliation of dismissal. His final production was an elegant account of *Love's Labour's Lost*. After fourteen years of exhausting work, Bridges-Adams deserved better.

With Bridges-Adams gone, the SMT was rarely distinctive. His replacement, Iden Payne,[17] deserved credit for maintaining Stratford's association with Komisarjevsky. He kept Bridges-Adams's best actor, Randle Ayrton, in the Company and recognised the talent of Donald Wolfit. The 1936 and 1937 seasons were the best of Payne's directorship. Komisarjevsky directed Ayrton in an acclaimed *King Lear*, Wolfit was admired as Hamlet, and eighteen-year-old Pamela Brown, who had just graduated from RADA, played Juliet and Cressida. All three left the company after the 1937 season. The board was content to sit on the money and run the company as if the new theatre had never been built.

2

The Post-War Years

Richard Burton and Claire Bloom photographed in 1955. Photograph: ZUMA Press / Alamy.

1 Barry Jackson

Archibald Flower suffered a stroke in 1941 and withdrew from public life. The Shakespeare Memorial Theatre remained open throughout the war, but the staff, left to their own devices, functioned like the servants of a great house when the master was away. They awaited the return of Archibald Flower's eldest son Fordham,[18] a lieutenant colonel in the army, serving in Europe and the Middle East. When Fordham Flower departed his regiment in 1945 there was never any question that he would succeed to all of his father's public positions, for decisions affecting the governance of Stratford-upon-Avon were astonishingly feudal and the Flowers were the lords of the borough.

Fordham Flower was as commanding a figure as his father had been in his prime, but he was more approachable and more willing to support new ideas. He was determined to make the SMT a playhouse of national importance. He wanted the best people and an ambitious programme and to this end appointed as director the distinguished and influential Sir Barry Jackson.[19] To announce the details of Jackson's first season, in January 1946, Flower invited the leading critics, players and producers of the London stage to a lunch reception at one of the capital's most exclusive palace hotels, the Savoy. As the guests finished the last course of a meal of classical French cuisine, perhaps Auguste Escoffier's Savoy dessert *Fraises à la Sarah Bernhardt*, and lit up their cigars, Fordham rose to tell them: 'The Governors have imposed upon themselves a little frank self-examination. There was a time when we were too prone to measure our achievements by the intake at the box-office, or the shape of the balance-sheet. Today, however, the Governors are determined that quality in acting and production should take precedence over profits.'[20] It was an effective public relations strategy. Most of the men Flower was addressing had shown little interest in Stratford over the years and certainly would not have travelled to the Midlands to attend a press conference. By inviting them to lunch at the Savoy, Fordham was changing perceptions of his theatre, and establishing goodwill.

Barry Jackson wasn't a young man, but his whole life had been filled with an enterprising and innovative spirit, and a belief that theatre should 'serve an art instead of making that art serve a commercial purpose'.[21] A Birmingham millionaire, passionate about the theatre from an early age, he poured his own money into the building of a new theatre for the company he founded out of an amateur group in 1912: the Birmingham Repertory Theatre. The Rep developed into arguably the most adventurous British theatre of the inter-war years. Jackson's personal wealth meant that he was able to take risks with the repertoire. The scope was extraordinary, mixing classic and modern plays and including rarities and the works of continental European writers. In the very first season, 1913, we find Shakespeare, Wilde and Granville-Barker, but also plays by Ibsen (*An Enemy of the People*), Arthur Schnitzler, Maurice Maeterlinck and Edmond Rostand. Although Jackson directed some plays, he was more a manager and facilitator of others. Once he chose a director he would support but never interfere.

The mainstays of the Rep were the plays of Jackson's friend Bernard Shaw, and of Shakespeare. Jackson introduced playgoers to the least well-known works, including the histories and the late romances, and his theatre was one of the first to present Shakespeare in modern dress. Among the future stars who appeared at the Rep at or near the beginning of their careers were Laurence Olivier and Peggy Ashcroft (aged nineteen, they appeared together in John Drinkwater's *Bird in Hand*, 1927), Gwen Ffrangcon-Davies (1921), Edith Evans (1923), Ralph Richardson (1925), Brenda Bruce (1936), and Margaret Leighton (1938).

Jackson saw exactly what was needed to reform Stratford. Crucially, he lengthened the festival and reorganised the structure of the seasons so that openings could be staggered to allow adequate rehearsal time; established workshops so that sets and costumes could be made on-site; brought in professional staff to manage the theatre (the elderly administrators who had run the theatre for decades were asked to retire – a horrendous moment for Fordham Flower who had known some of them since his childhood); and took with him from the Birmingham Rep the young Peter Brook and Paul Scofield. Brook had seen no potential in the Shakespeare Memorial Theatre when he'd visited it with Jackson before the latter started work. 'As we strolled through the trees,' he recalled years later, 'Sir Barry murmured, "This place could be as important as Salzburg." Poor old man, I thought to myself condescendingly, how could a dull English provincial theatre ever compete with the bold and sophisticated adventures that took place in that world called The Continent...' But Jackson went on to explain his plans, '...until in a few quiet phrases he had drawn the outline of what was to become the Stratford revolution that one day would put Warwickshire far ahead of Middle Europe.'[22]

Jackson didn't attempt to lure the biggest names to Stratford. Like Bridges-Adams before him, and Peter Hall fourteen years later, he believed in the ensemble, and wanted the actors he engaged to make long-term commitments to Stratford. 'The attitude of play a season, finish, begin again,' he wrote in *Theatre World* soon after his appointment, 'must be killed.'[23] Alongside Paul Scofield, he selected two players who were established but not household names – Robert Harris and Valerie Taylor. Surprisingly, he hedged his bets when it came to the directors. In case the ideas of Brook, directing *Love's Labour's Lost*, and Eric Cozier (who had recently staged the premiere of Benjamin Britten's *Peter Grimes* at Sadler's Wells), directing *The Tempest*, proved too shocking, he entrusted *Cymbeline* to the veteran Nugent Monck and *Henry V* to Dorothy Green, Benson's leading actress from before the Great War. When one of the junior players engaged by Jackson, Donald Sinden, arrived unshaven for the first rehearsal, Dorothy Green demoted him (cast as the Dauphin, he was told to play Grey instead).

The talking-point of Jackson's first season, 1946, was indeed Brook's *Love's Labour's Lost*, loved by the modernists but hated by the traditionalists. Brook's iconoclastic eclecticism, inventions (the Princess of France, played by Valerie Taylor, was accompanied by a mute white-faced Pierrot) and deliberate false notes (into the elegant *fête galante* setting ambled a British bobby carrying a truncheon and a string of sausages) were considered revolutionary at this address – memories of Komisarjevsky's productions were already fading. But the production had a haunting tone and Brook's handling of the ending turned the comedy on its head. 'The whole stage,' wrote Kenneth Tynan, 'had a wonderfully decadent *ancien régime* smell about it. The sudden change into the minor key at the end, when the tonic is replaced by a sudden diminished seventh on the entrance of Mercade with the news of the death of the Princess's father, came across as a superb dying fall, and left the actors twilit, their laughter frozen on their lips.'[24] Scofield became a star playing Don Armado. Unfortunately, the season lost money, the first to do so for many years. A small overspend on the annual budget didn't overly concern Jackson – the SMT had plenty of money in the bank – but those governors who disliked Jackson's modernising policies felt empowered.

In 1947, Brook directed *Romeo and Juliet* alongside a revival of his *Love's Labour's Lost* and the influential young director Michael Benthall arrived from London to stage *The Merchant of Venice*. *Romeo and Juliet* was the most anticipated production in the history of the SMT. Brook's search for two very young actors to play the title roles was covered in the press predictably enough, but it was Brook's focus on violence under a blazing sun, death in the afternoon, that would be remembered: his Mercutio was Scofield. Brook explained that, for him, it was a 'play of wide spaces in which all scenery and decoration easily become an irrelevance, in which one tree on a bare stage can suggest the loneliness of a place of exile; one wall, as in Giotto, an entire house. Its atmosphere is described in a single line, "These hot days is the mad blood stirring", and its treatment must be to capture the violent passion of two children lost among the warring fury of the Southern houses.'[25] The Stratford stage had never before been presented as an open arena, as stark as the cyclorama that rose above it. Brook's decision to cut the reconciliation scene alienated some of the critics. *The Guardian* concluded: 'Immense and accomplished work has gone into this production: it is certainly distinctive and challenging. But the final impression is, in a word, of a rather harsh *Romeo and Juliet*.'[26]

In planning his third season, Jackson, who was concentrating on the urgent work needed to renovate and modernise the building, asked Benthall to take on a bigger role. Benthall persuaded Anthony Quayle, another influential figure on the London stage, to join him at Stratford. In his usual manner of delegation and trust, Jackson gave these two friends the freedom to select actors and plays. Benthall would direct four of the productions, and Quayle two. It was a coup for Stratford to capture both Benthall and Quayle. Benthall brought in his partner Robert Helpmann and Diana Wynyard to lead the company, as well as a young actress who would become one of the biggest stars of the era – Claire Bloom, aged only seventeen. The most anticipated production of the season was *Hamlet*, directed by Benthall. It was decided that Helpmann and Scofield would share the title role. Bloom was cast as Ophelia, while Quayle chose to play Claudius. While there wasn't a production to rival Brook's *Love's Labour's Lost*, the work, collectively, had a consistency of tone, and an overall quality, that impressed. It was the first Stratford season to truly register nationally: there were interviews and picture spreads in glossy magazines and people travelled from London in large numbers to see the shows. Benthall set *Hamlet* in a sinister Gothic world of Victorian aristocrats. Bloom's Ophelia was turned into a sacrificial lamb. It was daring for the time. Perhaps Helpmann's saturnine, ageing and creepy Hamlet fitted the concept better than Scofield's young prince, but both succeeded. There were dissenting voices. The set made the critic of *The Guardian* think of Manchester Town Hall on a dark day.[27] The season was a triumph for Benthall but also for Jackson who had chosen the director and given him the space in which to work his magic.

During the planning for the season it became clear that all was not well. Jackson didn't pay much attention to the theatre's governors and was thought, by some, to be disrespectful. Flower may have reflected on Jackson's lack of diplomacy and dislike of gladhanding at the Savoy. Jackson's method of delegating, and giving the people he trusted ownership of their work, was misinterpreted by Flower as poor leadership. The underlying issue was that the two men were very different and didn't get on. 'I can't imagine that Fordie was ever very comfortable with the rather effete, mandarin-like Barry Jackson,' Peter Hall would write in his autobiography. 'Quayle's bluff "man among men" approach, bred of a good war and a keen ear, was far more his style.'[28] Flower was known to be furious when Jackson was slow to quash a malicious rumour that a man – Helpmann – was to be cast as Kate in Benthall's *The Taming of the Shew*.[29] At any rate, he was unable to establish a rapport with his aloof director and decided that someone of his own generation would be better equipped to continue the modernisation of the theatre. *The Times* suggested that Jackson's 'remoteness' was a problem for his actors and directors.[30] The paper's reporter was surely briefed by Flower or one of his underlings. It was a neat switch, a cunning way of diverting attention away from the Chairman and the board.

Jackson was denied the opportunity to develop the policies he had instigated. He may well have continued with Benthall and Brook as his associates, a tantalising thought. Brook believed that Jackson had been pushed out because 'although he knew every stagehand and cleaning lady and would stop daily to enquire about their ailments, when he met a governor, he could never remember his name'.[31] Brook made sure that Jackson's significance was not forgotten. In *The Empty Space* (1968) he wrote:

> When I first came to Stratford in 1945 every conceivable value was buried in deadly sentimentality and complacent worthiness – a traditionalism approved largely by town, scholar and press. It needed the boldness of a very extraordinary old gentleman, Sir Barry Jackson, to throw all this out of the window and so make a true search for values possible once more.

Although Jackson was only in charge for three seasons, he laid the foundations for all that followed. In the history of Stratford, there was before Barry Jackson and after.

Henry IV by Shakespeare, SMT, 1951. Richard Burton (Prince Hal). Production: Anthony Quayle. Design: Tanya Moiseiwitsch. Photograph: Hulton-Deutsch Collection / Corbis via Getty Images.

2 The Glamorous 1950s

Barry Jackson's departure was announced in January 1948, before the start of his final season. Flower selected Anthony Quayle to replace him, and allowed Quayle to take charge while Jackson was still technically in post. Flower admired and liked Quayle. He was a fellow soldier and had an officer's authority.[32] It was unclear whether Quayle had played a role in ousting Jackson. In his foreword to the handsome book of photographs by Angus McBean commemorating the 1948, 1949 and 1950 seasons, Quayle didn't mention his predecessor once.[33]

Anthony Quayle reinvented the actor-manager. He was confident, knowledgeable, a good Shakespearean; but also pragmatic, no-nonsense and committed to making a profit. Looking back in later life, he seemed to deny Jackson's achievement by describing the organisation he inherited as '[a] good old chug-along theatre'.[34] Quayle didn't share Jackson's aspiration to create a genuine ensemble. 'A wholly permanent company is neither desirable nor practicable,' he wrote.[35] He would later explain that it was undesirable because young actors shouldn't only perform one author's plays and impracticable because 'great stars cannot be expected to live permanently away from the West End…'[36] (in other words that Stratford would need a London home). These telling points would be addressed head-on by Peter Hall in 1961. Quayle's particular contribution was to make Stratford an extension of the London stage. He persuaded British theatre's greatest stars – John Gielgud, Michael Redgrave, Peggy Ashcroft, Ralph Richardson, Laurence Olivier – to take turns leading the company; and discovered Richard Burton and Ian Holm. Quayle was calling in friendships that had been formed back in the 1930s; and was helped by the goodwill of the West End impresario who effectively managed the careers of the big names, Binkie Beaumont. Quayle arranged for Beaumont to join the SMT's board. Because of the presence of famous actors, Quayle was able to make international tours a key element of his policy to increase Stratford's prestige and income.

These actors would not have come to Stratford if Quayle had not been able to complete Jackson's modernisation of the building. The proscenium was enlarged and the forestage extended. As importantly, as far as the actors were concerned, a green room and new dressing rooms were built on the river side (1951). Looking back in old age, Quayle would call the building 'a monstrosity' and express incredulity that the committee had chosen a design by a 'young woman'.[37] The improved building was one of Quayle's achievements (Tynan: '[It] retains its touching pink ugliness, but inside Quayle has made great changes, relining the auditorium to look warmer and more inviting'[38]); another was the 1951 'Festival of Britain' season, during which Shakespeare's *Richard II*, the two parts of *Henry IV* and *Henry V* were performed as an integrated cycle, with one designer, Tanya Moiseiwitsch, and in the belief that, as Quayle expressed it, 'the practice of presenting the plays singly had only resulted in their distortion… Their full power and meaning only became apparent when treated as a whole'.[39]

Moiseiwitsch designed a permanent wooden setting that took inspiration from the characteristics of the Elizabethan stage. Michael Redgrave played Richard II, Hotspur in the first part of *Henry IV* and the Chorus in *Henry V*, and directed the second part of *Henry IV*; Quayle took charge of the other three plays as well as excelling as Falstaff (he was always better suited to the character roles in Shakespeare than to the dramatic leads, a fact he acknowledged). Harry Andrews played Henry IV. The season was dominated by the charisma and voice of the young Richard Burton, playing Hal/Henry V. '[Burton's] playing of Prince Hal,' wrote Tynan in his review, 'turned interested speculation to awe almost as soon as he started to speak; in the first intermission local critics stood agape in the lobbies. Burton is a still, brimming pool, running disturbingly deep; at twenty-five he commands repose and can make silence garrulous. [...] He sits, hunched or sprawled, with dark unblinking eyes [...]. Burton smiles where other Hals have guffawed; relaxes where they have strained.'[40] The ensemble was strong. Alan Badel, a fine Fool to Gielgud's Lear during the previous season, played Poins. Michael Bates and Peter Halliday were Bardolph and Peto. Burton also played Ferdinand in Benthall's *The Tempest*.

For the first time in its history the Shakespeare Memorial Theatre was competing with the Old Vic for star actors; in fact, it often had the edge. Peter Brook's presence was a key part of Stratford's kudos, as was the arrival of a new young director, Peter Hall, in 1956. From the 1950s onwards, many young people who went on to have careers in the theatre caught the bug during their first visit to Stratford, with their family or school, sitting in the balcony or standing at the back of the stalls. In just a few years, thanks to Jackson and Quayle, the place acquired a powerful mystique. 'The safest introduction to the best in English theatre is still, for my money, the 2.10 from Paddington: change at Leamington for the shrine,' wrote Kenneth Tynan in 1952.[41] Gielgud's decision to work at Stratford was particularly important. Playing Angelo in *Measure for Measure*, he was transformed by Brook into a darker, edgier and less rhetorical performer than was felt possible. He played the title role in *King Lear* in his own production, and directed Peggy Ashcroft in *Much Ado About Nothing* and Ralph Richardson in *Macbeth*. Barbara Jefford, aged nineteen, played Isabella in Brook's *Measure for Measure*. The finest young actress of the Quayle years, she went on to play Lady Percy in *Henry IV* and Isabel in *Henry V* in 1951, Desdemona in 1952, Rosalind in 1953, and Kate in *The Taming of the Shrew* in 1954.

The rivalry that existed between Stratford and the Old Vic during the Quayle years was, for the directors, never acrimonious. Quayle seriously considered linking Stratford with the Old Vic to allow the two companies to swap theatres during the winter. For Quayle, the plan made practical and financial sense for both organisations, as well as being a means of helping his friends George Devine and Glen Byam Shaw, whose innovations at the Old Vic had been quashed by the theatre's board.

Both boards rejected the linking idea and instead Quayle invited the much-admired Byam Shaw to come to Stratford as his co-director. Quayle was feeling the strain of running the company while also directing and acting. Byam Shaw's arrival in 1952 allowed Quayle to step back from administration and to concentrate on performing. While Byam Shaw directed the 1952 Stratford season Quayle led a lucrative tour of Australia.

Glen Byam Shaw[42] had started his career as an actor and, like Quayle, knew most of the people worth knowing in the theatre. His friendship with Gielgud was established during their boyhoods at Westminster School, and their career paths often crossed. Byam Shaw played Benvolio in the celebrated Gielgud/Olivier/Ashcroft *Romeo and Juliet* at the New in 1935, and was a member of Gielgud's repertory company at the Queen's in 1937/38. After the war he retired as an actor to concentrate on directing.

The policy of building seasons around the biggest stars reached its peak in 1955 with the arrival of Laurence Olivier, making his Stratford debut. Olivier and Vivien Leigh played Malvolio and Viola in *Twelfth Night*, directed by John Gielgud, who had complicated feelings for both stars and was caught up in the ongoing crisis of their marriage, and Macbeth and Lady Macbeth, directed by Byam Shaw. These productions received poor reviews but satisfied the public. It only needed Olivier, as Macbeth, to leap athletically onto the banquet table for audiences to gasp. The season's one great production was Brook's *Titus Andronicus*. The play had never before been produced at Stratford and Flower and the board needed to be persuaded that it was suitable. This was a Peter Brook production in which Olivier played the leading role. Brook designed the sets and created an ominous soundtrack by using tape manipulation techniques, single drum beats and plucked strings. He had worked with Olivier, unhappily, on his film of *The Beggar's Opera*. This time he was determined to use the great talent and charisma of Olivier without losing absolute control. Every aspect was meticulously conceived and integrated. Brook used ritual and symbolism – naked flames; blood-red costumes and light; strips of ribbon to indicate spurts of blood – to give meaning to the play's succession of horrors. In Sally Beauman's description: 'It was as if the whole universe on stage had been drenched with blood. With every means at his disposal Brook played on the nerve-endings of his audience, but he played subtly.'[43]

Ian Holm, appearing in his second season at Stratford, played the small role of Mutius. 'Just being on stage, even for a few minutes,' he wrote in his autobiography, 'was a strange, almost frightening experience.'[44] Olivier was gracious but aloof, and surprisingly 'jittery' waiting in the wings to go on. He didn't tend to talk to junior members of the company off the stage, so Holm didn't get to know him at all until Olivier accidentally cut his finger with his sword and came to his dressing room with a bottle of

Scotch to apologise. Anthony Quayle, blacked up because he was playing the role of Aaron, joined them and before long Holm was legless. Holm wrote one of the best descriptions of Olivier in performance:

> The moment I felt compelled to watch from the wings every night, more often than not with tears in my eyes, was when Marcus asks Titus why he is laughing after a mountain of misfortune has been heaped upon him [...]. Olivier seemed to take an age to reply. He found a place on the stage directly beneath the most powerful spotlight and looked up straight into it. His harshly illuminated and magnified features betrayed resignation and extreme suffering, and he blinked several times into the intensity of the light as if about to weep. Once he had the audience expectant and thrilled, he began to speak, almost whispering the lines [...].[45]

As the National Theatre movement gained momentum, Quayle and Byam Shaw looked to strengthen the SMT's appeal for actors by finding a London theatre. This was not a first attempt to create the RSC. Quayle wasn't motivated by ideas on the nature of theatre, or by a desire to expand the SMT into a national theatre; on the contrary, he refused offers of state funding. What he did want was for an independent self-financing SMT to be considered the greatest Shakespeare theatre in the world, and this depended on its ability to continue to attract the finest actors. The fear was that once a state-funded National Theatre came into being in London these actors would no longer spend months on low pay in Stratford unless the SMT could offer them a presence in the capital as well. Fear of losing out to the NT was a recurring anxiety for Stratford, troubling its directorship in the early 1960s and the early 1970s.

George Devine agreed to join the directorate to run things in London. The scheme started to unravel when Devine left to create the English Stage Company at the Royal Court, and was abandoned when Quayle stepped down in 1956. Quayle felt that his work was done. He hated the idea of continuing for the sake of it, was bored with administration and eager to fulfil his potential as an actor in films.

Byam Shaw continued for a further three years. If he was never entirely happy in the role, he ensured that the SMT continued to prosper, an achievement underlined by the celebrated four-week tour of Russia in December 1958. Nevertheless, the lack of an ensemble ethos meant that many of the productions were neglectful of minor parts and came across as old-fashioned star-vehicles. The exceptions included the productions of Peter Hall. 'The stars policy had gone as far as it could,' Byam Shaw would admit years later. 'It had been done and overdone.'[46] Byam Shaw and Fordham Flower had recently decided that Stratford's future should be entrusted to Hall, and it was late one night in Leningrad, in a room in the Hotel Astoria, that the young director outlined to Flower his plan to transform the SMT into a national company.

A Midsummer Night's Dream by Shakespeare, SMT, 1959. Charles Laughton (Bottom), Mary Ure (Titania). Production: Peter Hall. Design: Lila De Nobili. Photograph by Tim Ring / Alamy. Previous page: Preparations at the SMT in December 1952 for the 1953 tour of New Zealand. Foreground: Barbara Jefford and her dresser. Photograph: Keystone Press / Alamy.

PART TWO

Dorothy Tutin speaking at an RSC press conference, Aldwych Theatre, January 1967. Photograph by J. Wilds / Hulton Archive, Getty Images.

3

Peter Hall

Peter Brook, Michel Saint-Denis and Peter Hall photographed at the RSC in March 1963. Photograph: *Daily Express* / Getty Images.

1 The Road to Stratford

Peter Hall was twenty-nine when he succeeded Glen Byam Shaw as director of the Shakespeare Memorial Theatre. His reputation was already formidable. As well as running the experimental Arts Theatre Club, he had directed Peggy Ashcroft, Laurence Olivier and Charles Laughton at Stratford, and Leslie Caron in the West End. He took charge of the SMT with the intention of creating a national company; remarkably, he achieved this bold, unlikely, and controversial *coup de théâtre* within a year. The hopes of Charles Flower would finally be realised. William Bridges-Adams had been defeated by circumstances and Barry Jackson by time; Hall succeeded. The man and the moment had finally merged.

Hall's father was a Suffolk stationmaster who moved along the railway line from Bury St Edmunds to Cambridge and finally to the village of Shelford. Hall attended the Perse, Cambridge's most prestigious school, where he edited the magazine, played Hamlet and rose to become head boy. A school outing to Stratford to see Peter Brook's production of *Love's Labour's Lost* (1946) initiated Hall's interest in directing. At Cambridge,[47] influenced by the English don George Rylands and by John Barton, his older contemporary, he started to formulate the ideas on textual analysis and verse-speaking that would become such an important feature of RSC performances. Barton and Peter Wood were the star directors. If Hall was in their shadow at Cambridge, he quickly overtook them out in the professional world.

His final student production, Pirandello's *Henry IV*, was reviewed in the London papers (1953). Alec Clunes, director of the

Arts Theatre Club, brought it to London for a two-week season. Within a month Hall found himself directing his first professional production, Somerset Maugham's *The Letter* at the Theatre Royal, Windsor. Alec Clunes had a word with his successor at the Arts Theatre, John Fernald, and Hall returned as a salaried assistant and script-reader while continuing to work as a guest director elsewhere. For six months in 1954 he ran the Oxford Playhouse.

The Arts Theatre mounted daring work, obscure classics and plays that could not be staged by 'legitimate' theatres because of the censor. Hall made his name directing bold productions of García Lorca's *Blood Wedding* (1954), an adaptation of André Gide's *The Immoralist* (1954), Ionesco's *The Lesson* (1955) and Julien Green's *South* (1955), and succeeded Fernald as director later that year. If Hall benefited from the support of influential people, he mostly made his own luck through the originality of his choices. His next production, *Waiting for Godot*, became the talking point of the theatrical year. He knew very little about Samuel Beckett when the play was sent to him in the post. The French version was playing in a small theatre in Paris. Hall knew that its originality would act as a provocation, never a bad thing for a young director. He staged it faithfully. The overnight notices were derisive, but Harold Hobson's glowing review at the weekend saved the day by proclaiming the play to be seminal. People rushed to the Arts Theatre to be part of this moment, and Hall became a public figure. The publicity brought him to the attention of Tennessee Williams (Hall staged *Camino Real* at the Phoenix in 1957) and of Stratford's Anthony Quayle and Glen Byam Shaw. Hall's rapid rise to celebrity status was consolidated by his marriage to Leslie Caron.

Overleaf:
David Warner and Helen Mirren photographed during the shooting of Peter Hall's RSC film of *A Midsummer Night's Dream*, 1967. Photograph: Trinity Mirror / Alamy.

2 Making the RSC

Ten years after seeing Peter Brook's *Love's Labour's Lost* Hall began his Stratford career with the same play (1956). *Cymbeline* with Peggy Ashcroft in 1957 and *Twelfth Night* in 1958, both designed with pictorial elegance by Lila De Nobili, were greatly admired. He became Glen Byam Shaw's chosen successor. Hall had wanted the Stratford job since his schooldays. A close relationship developed between the young director and Fordham Flower. By selecting Hall as director (the succession was settled informally by an exchange of letters), Flower was responding to the imminent birth of a state-funded national theatre under Laurence Olivier. However, when, during their midnight meeting in Leningrad's Hotel Astoria, Flower asked Hall to outline his detailed plans for the future he must have been taken aback by the young director's ambition: three-year contracts to create a genuine company, not just of actors but of directors and designers, the introduction of contemporary and experimental work, and – to make it all possible – a London base funded by the state. A national theatre in all but name, pre-empting Olivier's official troupe. The strategic and tactical ingenuity of this aspect of the scheme must have appealed to an old soldier like Flower. A new name, the Royal Shakespeare Company, would underline the Stratford Theatre's modernisation. By dawn Flower had agreed to gamble the SMT's reserves of £170,000 on the talent of Peter Hall and the expectation of an Arts Council grant.[48]

Hall was careful to reassure Flower by placing his revolutionary ideas within the context of the SMT's recent history. Flower knew that Hall valued the achievements of the organisation, and would build on the work of Byam Shaw and Quayle. Hall was happy to include star actors in the Company if they could fit in with the new ideas. Gielgud agreed to lead the 1961 ensemble but had a miserable time. The old hierarchies that separated stars from the rest were breaking down, at least at the RSC, and Gielgud, living in a

Cotswold cottage with his valet, found the process difficult. Hall had been so determined to bring Gielgud into the RSC that he had allowed him to choose the play, *Othello*, and the director, Franco Zeffirelli, and to approve Ian Bannen's casting as Iago. Zeffirelli's operatic production was extremely poor, an embarrassment for the actors and for Hall, who learned an important lesson. Gielgud responded with dignity, but his letters reveal that he blamed the director and particularly Bannen for the debacle.[49] He had a happier time appearing with Peggy Ashcroft in Michel Saint-Denis's *Cherry Orchard*.

Hall's concept of a permanent company was of a 'nucleus of actors who regarded [the] company as their permanent home, although they may go away from time to time in order to benefit from working in films and television'.[50] This was achieved (and would be sustained until the end of the 1990s). The time was right for the RSC. The name, as Hall predicted, appealed to people. William Gaskill congratulated Hall on the choice, telling him that it had everything in it but God.[51] The strength of Hall's ideas, provoking thousands of words in the newspapers, caught the imagination of the public and made the London adventure seem less of a gamble than it actually was. The passionate involvement of Peggy Ashcroft was of paramount importance. Other senior actors followed, but some were wary of the three-year contracts. Paul Scofield at first said yes, then changed his mind. Those who remained had to cope with an arrangement that divided their lives between Stratford and London. It was an adventure that vitalised nearly everyone involved. At the time, Hall wrote, 'a highly-trained group of actors, constantly playing Shakespeare, but with antennae stretched towards our world of contradictions, can, perhaps, be expert enough in the past and alive enough to the present to perform the plays...'; but he went on to add: 'However united a company may be, it is not automatically stable. If you are lucky enough to create it, it immediately begins to disintegrate... I suspect this is life. A company, like friendship, has to be constantly repaired.'[52]

To fulfil his plans, Hall needed to find a London theatre. At the beginning of the 1960s the West End was effectively controlled by three impresarios – Binkie Beaumont, Prince Littler and Prince's younger brother Emile. Binkie Beaumont, a Stratford governor, believed that Peter Hall would harm both the West End (by attracting away the best actors) and Stratford (by over-stretching resources) if he brought the RSC to London. He resigned from the board and did everything in his formidable power to prevent the RSC from obtaining a theatre. Prince Littler followed Binkie's lead. Hall played the rival Littler brothers off one against the other. He told Emile that Prince had turned him down. Emile promptly offered the Cambridge. Hall then returned to Prince, rightly predicting that he would change his mind to out-manoeuvre his brother. Prince offered the Aldwych, a theatre that suited Hall's purposes.[53] Hall obtained a three-year lease and the RSC opened in London at the end of his first Stratford season in December 1960.[54] Hall refitted the Aldwych so that it mirrored the changes he had made to the Royal Shakespeare Theatre – the stage was raked and extended far beyond the proscenium to form a new acting area that would allow some scenes to be staged close to the stalls. The Royal Shakespeare Theatre in particular, but also the Aldwych, were now epic theatres that, in the hands of the right director, could provide something close to intimacy.

Initially the RSC struggled to find a voice, despite the commitment of Peggy Ashcroft, Roy Dotrice, Dorothy Tutin, Max Adrian, Eric Porter, Derek Godfrey and Patrick Allen (among others) and the impact made by the young players Ian Holm, Ian Richardson, Diana Rigg and Judi Dench (among others). Peter O'Toole was a last-minute addition. Hall had persuaded Paul Scofield to lead the Company alongside Ashcroft. Scofield agreed to play Shylock, Petruchio and Thersites in *Troilus and Cressida*, but withdrew just a few weeks before the start of rehearsals. Peter O'Toole had just made a big splash playing Hamlet in Bristol and, luckily, was available. Hall would call O'Toole 'mesmeric' and 'really dangerous'. Casting such a young actor to play a role like Shylock was a risk. O'Toole told Hall that he believed in what he was trying to do with the RSC and was committed to the Company. He also said, when Hall asked him about his delicate new nose (he'd had a nose job since their last meeting), that he wanted to be a movie star.

O'Toole's young wife Siân Phillips accompanied him to Stratford and gave birth during the season. O'Toole dyed his hair black, grew a beard and was on top of his lines by the time rehearsals began, but he felt the pressure and drank even more heavily than usual. There was a heavy drinking culture in the theatre at the time; drinking was tolerated if it didn't affect performances. O'Toole wasn't the only actor to have a bottle of whisky in his dressing room or to take a swig in the wings, and late-night drinking sessions in the Dirty Duck pub were the norm. But O'Toole took things to extremes. Some of the younger actors followed him 'like seagulls following the plough'.[55] This worried Hall, who asked O'Toole to tone it down. While Peggy Ashcroft, Kate to O'Toole's Petruchio, was charmed by him, many of the senior players found him antagonistic and difficult to share a scene with. 'He acts at you,' Denholm Elliott said later.[56] Ian Holm, O'Toole's less flamboyant but greater contemporary, admitted that he had been 'terrified' by O'Toole: 'There was something unconsciously gladiatorial and threatening about him. O'Toole never seemed as if he could take direction.'[57] John Barton, director of *The Taming of the Shrew*, was used to student actors and didn't realise that directing Ashcroft and O'Toole required a higher level of tact. O'Toole objected to Barton's intellectualising and led a rebellion with Ashcroft's support. Hall felt that he had no choice but to take over the production.

The 1960 Stratford season opened with the early comedy *The Two Gentlemen of Verona*. The critical consensus was that the play was slight and the production lacklustre. It told the critics next to nothing about Hall's plans to create a company. O'Toole's performance in Michael Langham's *Merchant of Venice* was acclaimed, but it told the critics even less. O'Toole's performance was the last of the dominating crack-voiced star turns at Stratford, it belonged beside Olivier's Titus of 1955. It represented the end of the Stratford 1950s, not the beginning of the RSC 1960s. Hall's *Twelfth Night* divided opinion: Harold Hobson was one of the reviewers who expressed disappointment that Hall had revived an old piece of work. His review was typically brilliant, droll and eccentric, but in admiring Hall Hobson gave him no quarter and was deft at identifying paradoxes:

> One is all the more disappointed with Mr Hall for his apparently reckless disregard of his fame because his talents are so striking and so rare. There is no director in England who can penetrate

so surely as Mr Hall to the inmost meaning of a play, sometimes through words that might baffle a man with a less instinctive understanding of the drama. Yet, with all this brilliance, Mr Hall is subject to strange lapses. [...] Mr Hall's s principal weakness [is] that he pays both too much attention to words and too little. When he lets himself be impregnated by the entire spirit of a play, he is magnificent. But when he picks out certain phrases, and is cavalier in his treatment of the rest of the text, he does things that disquiet his friends. [...] The production [...] is lovely to look at. But nearly throughout Mr Hall treats it in terms, not of comedy, but of farce.[58]

Twelfth Night, created in the 1950s, was the work of a young director still finding his way. In contrast, Hall's next production, *Troilus and Cressida*, created with Barton, pointed to the future. It was revelatory because Hall and Barton identified the importance of Pandarus and Thersites, played by Max Adrian and O'Toole. Such was the significance of this moment that Hobson thought they had discovered something that Shakespeare had not been aware of, when, in fact, they were the first directors to rediscover the play he had written:

Peter Hall and John Barton have not been satisfied with academic explanations of the peculiar and contradictory aspects of *Troilus and Cressida*, its constant war between splendour of speech and grubbiness of action. As producers of the play they have found a theatrical basis for it, and so, perhaps for the first time in our history, made *Troilus and Cressida* not merely a collection of beautiful speeches, but a planned, architected, coherent, and powerful drama. [...] The producers have found the shape which Shakespeare himself missed; they have built upon a feeling that the universe is corrupt, and that worms triumph over nobility, a logical theatrical structure. The play contemplates lust and betrayal destroying grandeur. In the first part of the production, the spectacle is watched through the eyes of Max Adrian's clever and repulsive Pandarus with a lecherous, lip-licking lascivious delight. In the second part Pandarus almost vanishes, and his place is taken by the ragged and filthy Thersites, in whom the continuation of the story, as well as his own degraded nature, inspires a spiritually vomiting disgust. [...]

This use of Pandarus and Thersites is the framework which the producers have found for *Troilus and Cressida*.[59]

Hall's innovative decision to share the directorship, to make the Company an ensemble of directors and designers, was crucial. In 1962 Peter Brook, the acknowledged genius of post-war theatre, and the oracle-like Michel Saint-Denis, one of the century's most influential theatre artists (teacher, theorist and director), joined Hall as co-directors. 'We were a triumvirate of which I was the day-to-day chairman and manager,' Hall explained. 'We aimed to create an innovative Shakespeare company with techniques that were unmatched anywhere else.' Brook formed an experimental group; Saint-Denis established a workshop studio. Saint-Denis's role was limited by ill-health, but his presence was, for Hall, of paramount importance:

> What he gave to the Royal Shakespeare Company, and to me, its young founder, is incalculable. The company was callow, messy, bustling, adventurous, all over the place – and he, a man of great wisdom, decided to join the adventure. He gave me ballast and direction when it was critically needed. He spoke to the new ensemble of young actors about the European heritage, about Stanislavsky, Copeau and Brecht. But he did not give us cold theory. Michel hated dogma.[60]

Brook's influence, on and off the stage, was profound. Hall and Brook had first been linked by Kenneth Tynan, who wrote in *The Observer* in 1957: 'Having closely compared Peter Brook's [...] *Titus Andronicus* with Peter Hall's [...] *Cymbeline*, I am persuaded that these two young directors should at once go into partnership. I have even worked out business cards for them: – Hall and Brook Ltd., the Home of Lost Theatrical Causes. The present examples of Hallage and Brookery come unmistakably from the same firm. In each case the director has imposed on a bloodstained, uneven play, a unifying conception of his own.'[61] Brook would be the RSC's great innovator and truth-teller.

John Barton and Clifford Williams were associate directors; John Bury, from Joan Littlewood's Theatre Workshop, became head of design, supported by Farrah and Ralph Koltai. Harold Pinter became the Company's second house dramatist. Later, the young directors David Jones, Trevor Nunn and Terry Hands joined the team. Jones initially worked as an administrator at the Aldwych, and Hands headed the Company's touring wing, Theatregoround (1966). Hall and his colleagues challenged the traditions of the previous era, replacing painted cloths with three-dimensional sets, pictorial fantasy with realism, formless verse-speaking with a modern conversational style that, paradoxically, observed the iambic pentameter to the letter. This creation of a modern style of speaking Shakespeare was at the core of Hall's project. It was taught to the actors by Saint-Denis in the Studio, and by Hall and Barton in the rehearsal room. Hall told his actors in 1963:

> There is no mystique about Shakespearean verse. It is a craft that you can learn very quickly. It is in our new Studio that we want to tell you about line-structure, alliteration, rhyme, about rhythm and counter-rhythm, and the meaning of imagery. Some people believe that if an actor is true in the Stanislavsky sense, he will be led instinctively to the form of the verse. I don't believe this. An intelligent understanding of the form and expression of your text is as much the raw material of your creation as knowing the name of the character you are playing.[62]

Hall sought contemporary relevance in Shakespeare. Peggy Ashcroft, interviewed by David Addenbrooke in 1971, said of Hall: 'He had an academic's understanding of what Shakespearean verse is and he was anxious to have this verse spoken correctly and precisely. But he was also deeply concerned with what he believed was the overall conception of the play. Peter was very much interested in the political aspects of the plays.'[63]

'Going to the RSC is like going to university,' was something that actors often said, not always enthusiastically. They quickly realised that the RSC was a directors' theatre. Whereas the National under Olivier at the Old Vic was, first and foremost, a theatre for the actor, the RSC, centred on Hall, Brook and Saint-Denis, three artists who took an intellectual view of a play, quite naturally placed interpretation over performance.[64] In Hall's own words: 'If I had to choose between star actors making mincemeat of the play (and being brilliant themselves), and a director, with less good actors, revealing the play – I would choose the director.'[65] Hall's success in creating the RSC was the result of paradoxes. He was charismatic and charming, but could be blunt and ruthless. He valued collaboration, but was a benign dictator. He relished the political aspect of his role, the fight, but was worn down by it. 'I wish he'd stop pretending to be so bloody nice and simple,' remarked Glenda Jackson in 1967, 'when he's really very complicated and a dictator.'[66]

After a transitional year, the RSC started to fulfil Hall's vision with Saint-Denis's *The Cherry Orchard*, a production that united great stars and younger players – Peggy Ashcroft, John Gielgud, Dorothy Tutin, Judi Dench and Ian Holm – within the shared values of a recognisable company. Then came the remarkable 1962 season, in Stratford and London, where, alongside the Aldwych programme, Hall mounted seven small-scale productions at the Arts Theatre. Intimate accounts of Gorky's *The Lower Depths* and Middleton's *Women Beware Women* (directed by Anthony Page) were placed at the centre of a season of new plays. The most remarkable of these, David Rudkin's *Afore Night Come*, directed by Clifford Williams, was arguably the finest first play since John Osborne's *Look Back in Anger*. It was also gruesome and shocking and therefore 'an event'. On the opening night, as the severed head of an Irish vagrant, murdered by migrant farmworkers in a pear orchard, rolled across the stage towards the footlights, a spectator fainted, other spectators became restless and Harold Pinter told them to shut up and listen.

A few months later, two productions at Stratford persuaded the sceptical that something extraordinary was happening. Clifford Williams's *Comedy of Errors* was performed on a bare platform in the carnival spirit of *commedia dell'arte*. The cast entered the stage wearing contemporary clothes in grey; as the play progressed they added character-specific items of colour. Kenneth Tynan, who favoured Laurence Olivier and whose opinion of Hall and the RSC could be caustic, was convinced:

> *The Comedy of Errors* is unmistakably an RSC production. The statement is momentous; it means Peter Hall's troupe has

developed, uniquely in Britain, a classical style of its own. How is it to be recognised? By solid Brechtian settings that emphasise wood and metal instead of paint and canvas; and by cogent deliberate verse-speaking, that discards melodic cadenzas in favour of meaning and motivation.[67]

Less than a month later, Peter Brook's *King Lear* – a pitiless morally-neutral Beckettian howl of pain – opened with Paul Scofield in the title role. The last time Brook had created a production at Stratford, *Titus Andronicus* in 1955, he had been frustrated by the mediocrity of the younger actors; in 1962, he noticed a profound change. The young actors who were making *The Comedy of Errors* so riotously joyful, among them Alec McCowen, Diana Rigg, Peter Jeffrey and Tony Church, were also able to inhabit the bleak world of his *King Lear*. 'Watching this incomparable production,' Tynan began his review for *The Observer*, 'I cannot pretend to the tranquillity in which emotion should properly be recollected.'[68] Tony Church said of the production: 'This was one of the first really bare stage productions that we'd done, and in that sense it was seminal to a great deal of the work that's happened since. [...] I believe that *Lear* was the first example at the RSC of really breaking down a text and actually feeling the way into it. This has now become an RSC trademark.'[69] In 1963, the RSC performed *King Lear* in Paris at the Théâtre Sarah-Bernhardt, and in 1964 took both productions to Eastern Europe and America. Julie Christie joined the Company to play Luciana in *The Comedy of Errors*.

The RSC's future was secured by these productions and the quality of its work in the period up until 1966: Vanessa Redgrave in *As You Like It* (1962); Ashcroft, Holm, Donald Sinden, David Warner, Roy Dotrice, Eric Porter, Janet Suzman and Susan Engel in Hall and Barton's history cycle of 1963/64; the *Theatre of Cruelty* season (1964); Patrick Magee, Ian Richardson, Glenda Jackson, Michael Williams and Clifford Rose in Brook's *Marat/Sade* (1964); Holm, Vivien Merchant, Paul Rogers, John Normington and Terence Rigby in Pinter's *The Homecoming* (1965); and Warner, Glenda Jackson, Brewster Mason, Elizabeth Spriggs, Tony Church, Charles Thomas and David Waller in Hall's *Hamlet* (1965).

Pinter's presence proclaimed better than anything Hall's

transformation of the RSC into a theatre committed to new work. He had courted Pinter by staging a play originally written for television, *The Collection* (1962), and inviting the author to direct Patrick Magee, Brewster Mason, Bryan Pringle and Janet Suzman in a revival of *The Birthday Party* at the Aldwych (1964). Pinter's next work, *The Homecoming*, was duly delivered. Hall's associates were not convinced that the play would succeed on the main stage: 'Peter Brook thought the play too small for the large spaces of the Aldwych. So did John Barton. Michel St Denis felt that it was not poetic enough. Clifford Williams and Trevor Nunn were less specific, but neither said anything to stop the strong tide of objection.'[70]

Hall overruled his colleagues. His direction of the play matched the economy of the writing, as did John Bury's ash-grey set (the only colour was provided by a bowl of green apples on a sideboard). *The Homecoming*, about the struggle for dominance within an all-male London family and the disruption caused by the trophy wife one of the sons brings home from America, was deeply troubling in its exploration of human psychology, male and female, at its most basic level. The theme was elevated by Pinter's mastery of language, metaphors and ambiguity. A few people walked out most nights. When the show transferred to Broadway, the American producer, Alexander Cohen, told Pinter to 'fix the second act'. Hall recalled that: 'Harold took his glasses off, his eyes glinting. "What exactly do you have in mind?" he said. It was one of the few times I have seen a Broadway producer at a loss for words.' After *The New York Times* overnight review panned the play, Cohen told Hall that it wouldn't last the week. 'Do you really mean that?' Hall asked. 'Because if so, I was just setting up the next Stratford season and would be only too pleased to have *The Homecoming* actors in the Stratford company.' Enraged, Cohen shouted his reply: 'You have no right to talk about future plans. You have just had a flop on Broadway.'[71] Cohen had had his fill of these two arrogant young Englishmen. The production became a Tony Award-winning success despite the *New York Times*.

If Hall was right about David Rudkin, John Whiting, Peter Weiss and Harold Pinter (*The Homecoming* remains the most important play premiered by the RSC), he failed to recognise the talent of Tom Stoppard: *Rosencrantz and Guildenstern are Dead* was offered to the RSC but finally rejected by Hall after months of rewrites.

Hall led from the front with his own productions. His early Shakespeare work had been light-footed and romantic – the 1957 *Cymbeline* was conceived as a dark fairytale. The setting for *A Midsummer Night's Dream* (1959) was a Tudor banquet hall into which the forest ingeniously intruded. Titania was a young woman (Mary Ure); Puck, perhaps for the first time, was streetwise and sardonic (Ian Holm). *Coriolanus* (1959) featured Laurence Olivier at his most dynamic. Hall was adept at getting the best out of star actors, but his love of big performances played third fiddle to language and unity of tone. The 1960 *Troilus and Cressida* featured a sandpit and a rust-red cyclorama: the set made an appropriate visual statement while offering a bare arena for the actors. In the early 1960s Hall started to view the plays politically, projecting them through a lens of modernity. Working with John Bury, he developed a production style based on plain but emblematic imagery that complemented the psychological realism of the acting. From this an RSC house style emerged (minimal décor and furniture; a raked stage). Hall's productions of the *Henry VI* plays and *Richard III* (*The Wars of the Roses*) won acclaim for their narrative clarity and thematic cohesion, the central theme being the self-perpetuating brutality of power-politics. A dark, metallic environment was used to create the clamour of battle. In its austere setting and emblematic imagery, as well as its pitiless view of the human condition, the *Wars of the Roses* came from the same place as Brook's *Titus Andronicus* and *King Lear*. The 1965 *Hamlet* was a notable cultural event of the 1960s, the theatrical equivalent of a new LP by the Beatles.

The Wars of the Roses was the first part of a project to stage all of Shakespeare's English history plays in 1964. This unique event would celebrate the quatercentenary of Shakespeare's birth while making a huge statement about the RSC. Hall offered the project to Brook – 'You should always aim higher than yourself,' he wrote later[72] – but Brook was not interested in the plays at that time, and perhaps felt also that the project was the perfect fit for his friend. Hall was astute in casting Ian Holm and David Warner in the central roles of Richard of Gloucester and Henry VI. Neither actor was, at the time, an obvious choice. Holm – a loyal and unassuming company actor who had worked his way up the ranks at Stratford since 1954 – had been picked out and quietly supported by Hall from the beginning. Hall and Holm wanted a new approach to Richard, the opposite of Olivier's Machiavellian villain – deadpan, droll, and all the more chilling for being bureaucratic and seemingly ordinary. Considering why Hall chose him to play Richard, Holm wrote: 'My natural manner is one of complaisant civility, and if my performance could blend with this a sense of restrained but cumulative desire and striving, the result would be intriguingly fresh.'[73] After the reviews came out, Olivier wrote to Holm to congratulate him. Holm got the message: 'Essentially, he was re-staking his claim as the definitive Richard and, monstrously jealous, was making sure I understood who was boss.'[74]

Hall and Barton spent almost a year adapting the three *Henry VI* plays into two, cutting heavily. They believed that, in order to hold the attention of the audience and to emphasise the 'political ironies' that made the work universal, narrative clarity and speed were essential. As a result, they borrowed passages of text from Edward Hall's chronicles and even wrote new speeches in blank verse. Hall was uncomfortable with the approach and knew that Peggy Ashcroft would challenge it. He removed some of Barton's clever pastiches before the start of the rehearsals, but not all. Hall wrote later:

> Our adaptation, though well-intentioned, was indeed wrongheaded. [...] Once you start monkeying with original texts you start to put on a creative cloak yourself. [...] Most of the cutting and editing and rewriting of the classics occurs because we don't understand what the original is doing or – even more likely – are incapable of realising it. As a young man I didn't know it is better to work a little harder and a little longer than to cut.[75]

Hall, though, could not have worked any harder or longer. After a few weeks of rehearsal he broke down. The pressure Hall was under as he struggled to establish the RSC was real enough, but it was not the primary cause of his distress. Hall and Leslie Caron were still living together at their Stratford home, Avoncliffe, but she was frequently in Hollywood and their marriage was in the process of disintegrating. Hall had been suffering severe headaches and tiredness, but also sudden episodes of weeping. The death of John Whiting hit him hard. Holm recalled that Hall was carried into one rehearsal on a stretcher. Hall took to his bed and was told that electric shock treatment might be needed. He was ordered to stay off work for at least six months.

John Barton kept the rehearsals going and Peter Brook, who was working in Paris at the time, dropped everything and flew home. Brook believed Hall's doctor was wrong. He told Hall to go back to work immediately. Peggy Ashcroft agreed with Brook. Hall did as Brook said and found he could cope and that his sanity returned. He believed Brook saved his career.

The Wars of the Roses may have been, textually, something of a fake, but Hall's instincts were right. Audiences embraced the epic narrative as if it was a thriller and discovered along the way some of the young Shakespeare's greatest writing. Few people at the time even noticed the fake speeches. The RSC came into its own as an ensemble in these productions. The extraordinary performances were integrated within a collective style. 'The local doctor used to come round and give flagging actors a shot of Vitamin B12 in their bums, though I'm not certain we needed it,' wrote Holm in his autobiography. 'There was an extraordinary feeling of collective stamina, drive and energy as the unity of approach that ensemble playing required began to take hold and ripple through our ranks.'[76] Bernard Levin called the cycle 'monumental' and praised the 'attention to the verse and depth of the characters who speak it'.[77] The following year, Hall added *Richard II*, the two parts of *Henry IV* and *Henry V* and all eight Histories were performed in sequence.

Watching Warner's still, enigmatic Henry VI in the Histories, Hall knew he had found his Hamlet: 'He had that authentic quality stars always possess – they are completely watchable.'[78] Along with star-quality, Warner was an archetypal young man of the counter-culture 1960s. His Hamlet represented a decade that already felt remarkable and was marching towards *The White Album* and May 1968. Young people rushed to see the production. They identified with Warner's unconventional student Hamlet and with the production's central theme – the plight of the non-conformist in the face of an oppressive state. John Bury's shining black box set (made from Formica) consisted of two anterooms for spying. Many of the critics were less enthusiastic, objecting to the very thing that made the production noteworthy: they complained that Warner's Hamlet wasn't a prince. Harold Hobson, though, dismissed expectations based on convention and was 'excited, satisfied, beautifully astonished and profoundly moved' by Hall's 'offbeat' production.

> Hamlet is a man deeply unsure of himself, but he is not socially insecure. It does not occur to him to consider whether people approve of his long red undergraduate scarf or his bizarre clothes. [...] Mr Warner's Hamlet ignores convention, which is sufficiently an aristocratic thing to do, since it is only the established, the bohemian and the poor who can afford to do so without social and financial loss. What matters, of course, is [...] the inner authority. Mr Warner has that all right, and when the occasion demands he can interpret it in glittering physical terms. He may stoop from his outrageous height, wave his arms like a scythe, howl to the moon, and go after the king at a most unrefined gallop, but, if the immediate situation dictates it, he is spare, controlled, deadly, and most royally confident. [...] This *Hamlet*, then, is not only off-beat; it is better in intellect and emotion than any conventional interpretation one is likely to see for some time.[79]

Henry VI by Shakespeare, RST, 1963. Janet Suzman (Joan), Donald Sinden (York), Brewster Mason (Warwick). Production: Peter Hall. Design: John Bury. Photograph: Trinity Mirror / Alamy.

3   The Question of Subsidy

The RSC began its operation at the Aldwych, in December 1960, without having been able to settle the question of subsidy. Peter Hall knew that the Company would have to self-finance the Aldwych – which meant generating enough money at the box office – for an unknown length of time.

During the lead up to the move, Hall was extremely sensitive to any criticism. He revealed in his autobiography that he wrote to the editor of *The Sunday Times* to politely complain after Harold Hobson had used his notices of Stratford productions to repeatedly object to the policy of expansion. A critic of Hobson's stature could influence public opinion and weaken the Company's negotiating position with the Arts Council. Hall stressed the central importance of the move for the future of the RSC, and asked the editor to send his second critic to review the remaining Stratford productions of 1960. It was a time when newspapers and critics were still prepared to listen to directors. Hobson invited Hall to lunch at Prunier's. 'Over excellent fish,' Hall wrote, '[Hobson] said it had all been a misunderstanding; he simply enjoyed tweaking my tail. I was so serious about the move to London that a little mockery seemed in order.'[80]

Because Hall needed at least one major commercial success during the Aldwych's opening season, he programmed two plays with popular appeal, Giraudoux's *Ondine*, starring Leslie Caron, and Anouilh's *Becket*. *Becket* was a huge hit in Paris and Binkie Beaumont wanted to secure the British rights so that he could mount the play in one of his theatres. Hall personally lobbied Anouilh for the rights, knowing that the play would provide the Company with a financial lifeline. Anouilh agreed on the basis that Hall would cast his new star Peter O'Toole and Eric Porter in the leading roles of Becket and Henry II. However, O'Toole hadn't been kidding when he told Hall he was going to be a movie star. On one of his off days during the Stratford season, he'd met David Lean to audition to star in *Lawrence of Arabia*. Richard Burton and Albert Finney had turned down the part and Lean was determined to cast O'Toole. O'Toole was just as determined to say yes despite his commitment to the RSC – he was under contract to play Henry II, Petruchio and Shylock at the Aldwych. Hall refused to release O'Toole. He feared losing *Becket*. Sam Spiegel, producer of Lean's film, would not even agree to a short delay to allow O'Toole to appear for a few weeks at the Aldwych. Let them sue, O'Toole was told. The RSC didn't have the finances to risk legal action, and, anyway, Hall knew that if O'Toole wanted to go he was of no use to the RSC. O'Toole was completely in the wrong, but it seems he held a grudge against Hall: when someone handed him a copy of Hall's autobiography he ripped it in half.[81] Hall was able to retain *Becket* and save his Aldwych season because Christopher Plummer agreed to join the Company to play Henry II, followed by Benedick and Richard III at Stratford. O'Toole's departure wasn't an issue going forward. A theatre troupe could only really tolerate a personality as big as O'Toole's for a short time. A project like *The Wars of the Roses* was only possible because the players believed in the ensemble.

Becket and *Ondine* were glamorous and very well done but somewhat anomalous. John Whiting's *The Devils*, the RSC's first commission, was more in line with the ethos of the Company.

While all this was happening, Hall continued to press the Arts Council to allocate to the RSC the annual subsidy that would enable the Company to remain in London. The process was tortuous.[82] The leaders of the National Theatre movement, realising that Hall was transforming Stratford into a national theatre and seeking public funding, had brought the RSC into their orbit, inviting Hall and Flower in 1960 to join the executive committee of the Joint Council of the National Theatre, led by Oliver Lyttelton (Lord Chandos). The Old Vic was represented by Michael Benthall and the West End by Binkie Beaumont and Prince Littler. The committee was charged with submitting proposals to Lord Cottesloe of the Arts Council and to the Treasury.

The situation was delicate for both sides. Chandos and his supporters feared that the RSC would become the National by default;

that the government would grant it this status and hand it all of the money earmarked for the building of the National Theatre, which would be abandoned. The RSC feared that it would be allocated no money at all if the government remained committed to the Nation Theatre project. Both sides, therefore, saw the benefits of a merger. Hall went so far as to agree that once the National Theatre building opened, the RSC would, along with the Old Vic, be absorbed into the National and would give up its independence, assets and separate governing structure. The context, though, was that the RSC needed a subsidy immediately and feared that the only way of getting it was to go along with the merger idea. The reality of merger seemed far off since the National Theatre building still needed to be built. It seems that Hall and Flower initially hoped that they would rule the new organisation, but it soon became clear that Laurence Olivier would be placed in overall command.

For a brief time it looked as if Stratford would become the National Theatre by default. The Macmillan government suddenly announced that it was abandoning the scheme to establish a new National Theatre and instead would assign all of the money, as annual subsidies, to Stratford, the Old Vic and regional theatres. It is unclear whether Hall had been aiming for this result all along – he later denied it; but the moment went to his head: he submitted a three-year plan that required £124,000 plus £400,000 to radically alter the Royal Shakespeare Theatre.

However, Lord Chandos was not of the character to give up. The London County Council (the precursor to the GLC), dismayed by the government's decision (the council had allocated a site on the South Bank for the new building), told the Chancellor, Selwyn Lloyd, that it would allocate £1,300,000 if the government honoured the terms of the National Theatre Act of 1949 by releasing £1,100,000. The National Theatre was back on, but now the Arts Council and the Treasury wanted to establish an opera house as well as a theatre on the South Bank. The RSC was told that if it didn't agree to be absorbed entirely into the National Theatre it would receive no funding of its own, not even during the long period before the National Theatre was built and opened.

This was in the summer of 1961. Arnold Goodman was asked by Chandos to write the constitution for the National Theatre.

When he arrived in Stratford, Hall and Flower sent him packing. He later told Hall that his 'humiliation was so great he ought to have travelled back to London disguised as a washerwoman'.[83] Hall and Flower were not prepared to go along with what they decided was a policy of coercion. They now told Chandos that they would only consider a system of cooperation that would allow the RSC to remain independent. Chandos therefore removed the RSC from the new plan he submitted to the Treasury. Hall and Flower believed that Olivier and Chandos were actively lobbying against them, and they were wary of Lord Cottesloe, a long-term supporter of the National.

In March 1962, Hall launched a press campaign on behalf of the RSC, and Flower lobbied the government through the MP for Stratford, the soon to be infamous John Profumo. Interviewed by *The Daily Telegraph*, Hall said:

> If the support from the Treasury does not materialise then I fear that we will not only be forced to give up the Aldwych and the Arts theatres in London, both absolutely essential to our policy, but that the Shakespeare seasons at Stratford will suffer fatally through being unable to compete with a highly subsidised National Theatre.[84]

The Telegraph published the story under the headline 'Fears for survival of Royal Shakespeare'. Articles in most of the other papers followed, all of them calling on the government to support the RSC. On 9 July, the country's leading theatre critics published a letter in *The Telegraph*, in which they wrote:

> There is a great danger that the RSC may have to cease its London productions [...] unless the company is given either an immediate grant of public money or at least a firm promise of one very soon. We would like to affirm, unanimously, our belief in the vital importance of the company to the life of the London theatre [...] Any setback to halt its activities would in our view be a disaster.[85]

The letter was signed by Felix Barker, Alan Brien, W.A. Darlington, Bamber Gascoigne, Harold Hobson, Philip Hope-Wallace,

Bernard Levin, Robert Muller, Milton Shulman, Kenneth Tynan and T.C. Worsley. Worsley, in *The Financial Times*, implicated the National Theatre, writing that its leaders (which, for the public, meant Olivier, recently confirmed as its director) wanted to expel the RSC from London. Olivier, stung by the adverse publicity, went to see Hall and Flower in Stratford, offering the RSC an annual three-month season at the National. There was confusion, though, as to whether he would require them to relinquish the Aldwych as a result.

A few days later, on 31 October, the Arts Council suddenly announced that the RSC would be granted a subsidy of £47,000 for 1963/64. While this was a relatively small amount, less than a fifth of the sum earmarked for the National, it was a huge relief for Hall and Flower: the principle had been won and the RSC could continue. It is hard to know whether Hall and Flower's publicity campaign was decisive or whether the Arts Council was always, in the end, going to support the RSC; but resentment over Hall's *fait accompli* lingered for years within the Arts Council. Hall committed the Company's future to the City of London's Barbican Arts Centre, then being built.[86]

Hall's risk-taking was apparent in all aspects of his management of the RSC and greatly contributed to the Company's success. It was there in his casting of young actors like Peter O'Toole and David Warner in leading roles, in his support of Peter Brook's experimental work, in his decision to devote an entire season to the history plays (epic cycles of this kind were new in Britain), and in his taking-on of the censor, the Arts Council and the National Theatre. Hall provided a neat and tidy summation of the 1960-62 merger negotiations in his autobiography:

> There was a sense that both theatres were competing for the future, and this was much played on by the media. My passion was Shakespeare, and the RSC was where I belonged. My aim was for the RSC to be recognised and properly funded so as to be equal in resources with the NT. Larry wanted the NT to be pre-eminent – to pay more, spend more and mean more. And his views were shared by many in the Establishment.[87]

This was too simplistic a statement to be read at face value. Hall may well have been content with an equal share of the resources, but he wanted the RSC to be pre-eminent.

Above: Diana Rigg in 1965. Photograph: Trinity Mirror / Alamy.
Left: *Henry V* by Shakespeare, RST, 1964. Ian Holm (Henry V). Production: Peter Hall and John Barton. Design: John Bury. Photograph: Trinity Mirror / Alamy.

4 Michel Saint-Denis

By bringing in Michel Saint-Denis and Peter Brook, Hall ensured that the RSC was international, ideas-driven and radical.

It is hard to think of an important English classical actor of the middle decades of the 20th century who was not influenced, either directly or indirectly, by the great French director and teacher Michel Saint-Denis. Saint-Denis survived the Great War and spent the formative years of his career with his uncle Jacques Copeau's company at the Théâtre du Vieux-Colombier in Paris. Initially Copeau's secretary, he acted, directed and wrote plays in collaboration with Jean Villard. In 1930 he formed his own troupe, La Compagnie des Quinze.

La Compagnie des Quinze caused a sensation when they visited London in 1931. Saint-Denis's highly stylised direction and the physicality of the acting – utilising masks, mime and music – inspired many young actors and directors, including Michael Redgrave,[88] Peggy Ashcroft and John Gielgud. Working in England from 1935, the year he founded the London Theatre Studio, Islington, Saint-Denis advocated permanent companies and in-house training and taught a method of creating theatre that was essentially new on this side of the Channel. Insisting upon long rehearsal periods, the autocratic Saint-Denis looked for truth and meaning in improvisation; he believed that reality on the stage depended on the discovery of a collective style, and expected his actors to bring to the work everything in their experience of life. Between 1935 and 1937 he directed John Gielgud in *Noah* (New Theatre), Edith Evans in *The Witch of Edmonton* (Old Vic), and Laurence Olivier in *Macbeth* (Old Vic), but it was not until 1938, at the Queen's Theatre and then the Phoenix Theatre, that the benefits of his approach became clear. John Gielgud, Peggy Ashcroft, Michael Redgrave, Alec Guinness, George Devine and Glen Byam Shaw were asked to work together on each play for seven weeks and to consider the smallest of details. The result was Saint-Denis's *Three Sisters*, a production widely acclaimed as an ensemble masterpiece.[89] Although the outbreak of the war cut short this important episode, there can be little doubt that it inspired Gielgud to base his theatre work of the 1940s and 50s around repertory seasons, and left Ashcroft looking for the theatrical home she would eventually find at the RSC.

During the war Saint-Denis ran the BBC's French section. His radio broadcasts entered millions of French homes and offered hope and encouragement to all those who felt crushed by the Occupation and Vichy.[90] In 1946 he started again. He was general director of the Old Vic Theatre Centre until 1951.[91] In this capacity, he oversaw the reconstruction of the stage and auditorium and directed Olivier in *Oedipus Rex* and Ashcroft in *Electra*. Between 1952 and 57 he was back in France, the first director of the Centre National Dramatique de l'Est in Strasbourg. At the end of the decade he helped to establish the National Theatre of Canada in Montreal and the Juilliard Drama Division in New York.

Peter Hall's conversations with Saint-Denis during the 1950s crystallised his own thoughts about theatre companies.[92] By asking Saint-Denis to join the RSC and to direct Peggy Ashcroft and John Gielgud in *The Cherry Orchard* (1961), Hall was making a particular statement about the significance and role of his new company, and it is appropriate to view the RSC of Hall, Brook, Ashcroft and Saint-Denis as the final destination of 20th century English theatre. For Ashcroft, Saint-Denis was 'the most instructive director that I have ever worked with, but his form of direction is, in a sense, one hesitates to say "of the past", but it isn't the way in which actors are now used to working in the theatre'. She went on to compare Saint-Denis's approach to that of his younger colleagues: 'With Michel, it was the direction of a master. He worked on the system that the director has planned his whole production from A to Z. And one knew that *he* knew what the whole was supposed to be. On the other side, if you take Peter Hall, or Peter Brook, I think they would say that a play is an adventure, an experiment, an unknown – and we'll discover it together.'[93]

Saint-Denis's particular RSC task was to set up and run a centre for experimentation and training (the Studio), but he also acted as

Hall's confidant. In his autobiography Hall depicts Saint-Denis as a figure of wisdom who provided 'direction'. Saint-Denis viewed the theatre, as he viewed life as a whole, in a very principled way. From Saint-Denis, Hall learned that the director of a great theatre had a duty to the paying public to strive to place before them something extraordinary, every single night.

> He felt [...] that all of us in the theatre should not just display whatever talents we may have to their best advantage, but also be at our best as people. [...] Everything he did in the theatre was based on cherishing the quality of the human being. [...] An actor had to use acting not to hide himself, but to reveal himself.[94]

The Studio had a brief but significant history. It was initially a marquee in the garden of Avonside (the artistic director's house); later, a temporary building was erected on waste ground in Southern Lane. The purpose of the Studio was to discover a modern style of producing Shakespeare. Saint-Denis's own explanation, written in 1963, reveals the intellectual approach, and pioneering spirit, of the RSC's first directors:

> The modern theatre is roughly divided between two movements. One, the newer, is the result of many complex tendencies. The other is the mass of traditional theatre, from the Greeks to Chekhov. This movement believes in the virtues of form and style to express reality or to transcend it. With Shakespeare in Stratford we are looking after the highest form of traditional expression in the modern theatre. All over the world, most of Shakespeare's work is recognised as having the greatest contemporary value from the point of view of meaning as well as of form. Shakespearean production must renew itself with much more daring and evidence. The Royal Shakespeare's main line of action has the essentials for a theatrical enterprise of artistic ambition. These are the making of a Company working together over the years, their development and yearly renewal – actors, directors, technicians, playwrights – based on a Studio for further training and experiments. In addition, Peter Hall and Peter Brook share my belief that Shakespeare stands as a popular force actual enough to illuminate the modern scene if the

modern passion for 'reality' can be fed and expressed by him; and that a re-examination of the nature of Shakespearean poetry, of its style, of its direct power to reveal reality in modern terms, is an urgent need if the interpretation of Shakespeare is to be brought up to date. The Studio we have created is intended as the instrument of this re-examination. Its function is to conduct experiments through which a contemporary way of producing Shakespeare and the Elizabethans, and other styles as a consequence, can be prepared.[95]

In practical terms, this meant the training of actors in technical skills such as verse-speaking and movement, but also the stimulation of the imagination through knowledge, discussion and improvisation. All company members had access to the Studio, but it was the youngest actors who benefited the most. Saint-Denis's language may seem high-flown today, but the thinking, shared by Hall and Brook, was crucial to the RSC's achievement in forming a style and an identity that would last long after Saint-Denis's retirement and the closure of the Studio in 1966. The tin hut would be reborn as the Other Place theatre in 1974.

Overleaf:
Glenda Jackson photographed in Stratford in March 1965.
Photograph: Mirrorpix / Getty Images.

5 Peter Brook

Peter Brook accepted Peter Hall's invitation on condition that he could form a group that would operate outside of the formal structures and deadlines of the Company. Brook wanted theatre-making to be a collective endeavour and an evolving process.

Brook had been at the forefront of the British theatre since the age of twenty. The son of scientists, both of Russian origin, both distinguished, he was brought up in Chiswick, west London. He went to prestigious schools (Westminster, Gresham's and Magdalen College, Oxford) without having much liking or use for them, and was just too young to fight in the war. And yet, for whatever reason, he was a young man in a hurry who possessed from the beginning those technical and managerial skills of the theatre normally only acquired through experience.

If the young Brook was a theatre man waiting in the wings – he has written that when he first went to the theatre his interest was held not by the play but by a curiosity in the unseen backstage activity that made it happen[96] – what he wanted most was to make films. He left school at sixteen to take up an apprenticeship at Merton Park Studios in south London, but quickly found the work boring and unglamorous. He learned that becoming a film director meant many years of hard graft climbing the industry ladder, whereas play directing could be achieved through personal enterprise and guile. Going up to Oxford in 1942[97] he directed – in a hired theatre near Hyde Park Corner in London (the university theatre society was a closed shop) – a student production of Marlowe's *Doctor Faustus*. However, he found that he could not give up his ambition to make films. With a group of fellow enthusiasts he shot a movie of Laurence Sterne's *A Sentimental Journey*. This was the first example of Brook's extraordinary ingenuity and drive. He circumvented the wartime ban on the selling of film by purchasing rejected stock from the RAF, and the ban on commercial developing by employing a Soho pornographer. It was Brook's impudence, as much as the illegality of the project, that led his college to threaten to send him down unless he abandoned directing for good (amusingly, the dons made him sign such a declaration). Within months of graduating he achieved fame in the theatre. He would return to movie making, directing Laurence Olivier in *The Beggar's Opera* (1953), Jeanne Moreau and Jean-Paul Belmondo in *Moderato Cantabile* (1960) and, most notably, an adaptation of William Golding's *Lord of the Flies* (1963), but it would never become his metier.

Brook made his name in a small theatre in an unassuming street behind a station in Birmingham (perhaps he had a sense of coming full circle when, decades later, he entered another theatre behind a station – the Bouffes du Nord). Without Barry Jackson, director of the Birmingham Rep, who took a risk on the young director, and Paul Scofield, the actor who starred in those first remarkable productions, his career might have taken longer to ignite. *Man and Superman*, *King John* and *The Lady from the Sea* (1945) signalled a generational change. Brook directed without reference to tradition, concentrating on interpretation and visual inventiveness and curbing the actors' long-established propensity for melodrama and bombast, and it was perhaps surprising that he took so many with him (the actress Mabel France remarked to Jackson, 'That young man knows what he wants, and he is going to get it'[98]). The following year Jackson engaged Brook to direct *Love's Labour's Lost* at Stratford. Few critics had seen the Birmingham work, so it was Brook's fresh take on *Love's Labour's* – the charm, mystery and melancholy of a Watteau painting, but with provocative anachronisms – that established his reputation as the wunderkind of the English stage. It was after the opening of *Love's Labour's Lost* that Brook met Michel Saint-Denis for the first time. Saint-Denis had seen the production and took the opportunity to give the young director some advice. 'He sat back in his chair, pulling on a pipe,' Brook writes in his autobiography, 'and explained that it was a great mistake to imitate famous paintings, as the theatre is theatre in its own right and true theatre art should not refer to anything outside itself.'[99] At the time, Brook was enraged by the criticism.

Throughout the 1950s Brook was something of a jack-of-all-trades, always on the move, a mountebank carrying in his suitcase a box of tricks that delighted audiences at Covent Garden, in the West End and at Stratford (he would exhaust his interest in theatrical devices by the end of the decade). His originality was most apparent in his productions of Shakespeare, particularly of the then little-known *Measure for Measure* and *Titus Andronicus* at Stratford in 1950 and 1955. The theatre of the immediate post-war years understandably sought to offer escape and fantasy. Brook, though, brought the contemporary Europe of police states, paranoia and fear into his versions of *Measure for Measure* – interpreted as a play about government and society rather than as a problem comedy – and *Hamlet* (1956). The latter formed the central part of a season of plays with Scofield at the Phoenix Theatre that seemed connected by these themes (an adaptation of Graham Greene's *The Power and the Glory* and T.S. Eliot's *The Family Reunion* completed the repertory). The 1955 rediscovery of *Titus Andronicus*, starring Laurence Olivier, was Brook's most flamboyant classical production.

Peter Hall's invitation came at a time when Brook was restless for something new. He had come to see the 'absolute truth'[100] of Saint-Denis's criticism. As far as Shakespeare was concerned, Brook believed that the modern world had yet to catch up:

> For centuries our practical understanding of Shakespeare has been blocked by the false notion that Shakespeare was a writer of far-fetched plots which he decorated with genius. Today we are beginning to see that Shakespeare forged a style in advance of any style anywhere, before *or since*, that enabled him to create a realistic image of life. Shakespeare, knowing that man is living his everyday life and at the same time is living intensely in the invisible world of his thoughts and feelings, developed a method through which we can see at one and the same time the look on the man's face and the vibrations of his brain. Our problem is to bring the actor towards an understanding of this remarkable invention, this curious structure of free verse and prose which a few hundred years ago was already the cubism of the theatre. We must move the productions and the settings away from all that played so vital a part in the post-war Stratford renaissance – away

from romance, away from fantasy, away from decoration. Now we must look beyond our outer liveliness to an inner one.[101]

Brook directed Paul Scofield in a production of *King Lear* (1962) that coldly discarded over a century of performance tradition. The setting was bare, off-white and plain. Tall panels were used for the interior scenes; an empty stage for the rest. During the storm scene, three large sheets of rusting metal reverberated above the bare stage. Bright white lighting was used throughout, and there was little music. Brook suggested to Scofield that the play amounted to a relentless process of stripping away. Lear must be deprived of everything, including Cordelia. Scofield didn't disagree, but said that it didn't help him as an actor because he couldn't play a negative action.[102] Scofield's Lear was an implacable autocrat who wrecked lives, a bully with cropped hair, physically threatening, very much the author of his own fate. Famously, the phrase 'I shall go mad' was delivered not as a premonition but as a warning. Brook viewed the play as the 'epic unfolding of the nature of the absurdity of the human condition'. After the storm Lear became a figure of desolation and of the grotesque. Shakespeare as a precursor of Samuel Beckett – this was greeted as a revelatory moment in the performance history of Shakespeare, although the idea had been explored by Jan Kott in *Shakespeare Our Contemporary*, published as Brook was working on the production. In interviews Brook expressed the belief that a production should challenge, provoke and even disturb, and his RSC productions had an intensity that set them apart. At the core of the new work was the feeling that the director should not rely on devices; that the process should be about releasing the 'infinite possibilities within the actor'.[103] In rehearsals and on the stage Brook introduced disorder, surprise and rough edges in an attempt to make dramatic performance truer to life.

After *Lear*, Brook agreed to direct *The Tempest* to open the 1963 season. His mind, though, was elsewhere. Brook and Hall were alike in many ways, but their approach to actors was different. At this time, Brook was feared by some actors: he could be intimidating and was quick to lose his temper. 'There was no gentleness about him,' recalled Holm, cast as Ariel. 'He was a *puppetmeister* in a different way from Hall, who had a way of disguising or at least softening the means whereby he achieved his ends.'[104] When Brook was 'particularly foul' to the young actress playing Miranda, Philippa Urquhart, his Prospero, Tom Fleming, took him to task in front of the company. Brook stormed out of the production.[105] Hall asked Clifford Williams to take over. Understandably, the reason for the change of director wasn't made public. Instead, the RSC presented the production as if Brook and Williams had collaborated from the start.

By 1964, Brook had set up his own dedicated group. Aided by Charles Marowitz, he selected ten young actors, all new to the RSC, and devised the exercises and improvisations that evolved into the *Theatre of Cruelty* performances at LAMDA in 1964.[106] Brook was new to experimental techniques and relied on Marowitz's practical expertise. The performances consisted of animal-like noises; nonsense sketches (by Paul Ableman); Artaud's three-minute piece *Spurt of Blood*; Alain Robbe-Grillet's short story *Scene*, told only in movement; a collage by Brook called *The Public Bath*, in which Glenda Jackson, the only major performer to emerge from the group, was washed in a tin bathtub and dressed in a prison smock to the accompaniment of readings from reports of the Christine Keeler case and the Kennedy funeral; *The Guillotine*, another collage; John Arden's short play *Ars Longa, Vita Brevis*; the *Marowitz Hamlet*; and improvisations that changed nightly. It is difficult, for the outsider, to gauge the exact value of all this. The point is that Brook took what he needed from Marowitz (and others) and then moved on. By the end of the year he had expanded the group to perform Jean Genet's *The Screens* at the Donmar Rehearsal Studios and taken the workshop aesthetics and many of the visual ideas of the *Theatre of Cruelty* project into the creation of his great production of *Marat/Sade*[107] at the Aldwych.

Peter Weiss's play, in which the Marquis de Sade, imprisoned in the asylum at Charenton in 1808, directs his fellow inmates in a play about the murder of Marat by Charlotte Corday during the Revolution, was, for Brook, one of the few contemporary works that had the scale and ambition of an Elizabethan or Jacobean play. As importantly, it stressed the value of images, music and sound, incorporated modernist thinking from Artaud to Genet via Brecht, and juxtaposed opposing styles to create a dialectic that was richly dramatic. The experimental group came together with leading players from the main company, including Ian Richardson and Patrick Magee. The actors visited mental hospitals and prisons, and were asked by Brook, dangerously, to explore their own experiences of mental disquiet (Morgan Sheppard: 'One wasn't quite able to cope with one's own inner violence and nastiness';[108] Glenda Jackson: 'We were all convinced that we were going loony').[109] *Theatre of Cruelty* bled into *Marat/Sade*. The exercises on non-verbal means of expression resulted in a depiction of lunacy that was realistic in the extreme. The tin bath and the guillotine reappeared.

The visual language of *Marat/Sade* was compelling. A circle of sunken baths, at times covered by wooden boards, formed the central feature of Sally Jacob's stark design. Grotesque white faces emerged from the pits, marshalled by nuns and guards. A group of the inmates, with painted clown-like faces, formed a satirical singing chorus. Others were dressed up in the red caps and *tricouleur* rosettes of the Terror. The disruptive were beaten or forced upside down and doused with water. Patrick Magee's Sade observed and directed with a cold sense of detachment. Glenda Jackson's half-asleep inmate (playing Corday) leant against a wall, her head lolling sideways to reveal the vulnerability of her neck. Brook created a theatre piece that assaulted the senses as much as the intellect; within a riot of noise and physical movement he focused attention on certain objects and faces and created images inspired by Goya and David. One such image was Glenda Jackson's extended bare arm holding the knife above Marat's chest. Many people had viewed the *Theatre of Cruelty* work performed at LAMDA as self-indulgent and purposeless; when *Marat/Sade* opened its purpose become clear.

The anti-establishment aspects of Brook's radical RSC came to the fore when he developed the theatre piece *US*, a condemnation of American policy in Vietnam. A year in preparation, fifteen weeks in rehearsal, this radical statement of protest against the war opened at the Aldwych in October 1966. Words, songs, movement, a montage of disturbing images and sounds, the repetitive expression of rage and pity – Brook and his collaborators set out to shock, provoke, and to end detachment. During the last few minutes of the show, butterflies were let loose in the auditorium. Michael

Williams held a butterfly between his fingers and set it on fire with a lighter.

As a piece of theatre, *US* was somewhat pretentious. Brook instructed the actors to silence any applause. This provoked a long awkward silence, during which the actors placed brown paper bags over their heads. On the opening night, Peter Cook shouted from the circle, 'Are you waiting for us, or are we waiting for you?' The burning of the butterfly, as intended, caused outrage. The butterfly, though, was a piece of paper. The RSC told the RSPCA but not the press.

In 1970 Brook returned to Shakespeare. In directing *A Midsummer Night's Dream* in an abstract white box, with elements taken from the circus, he dismissed romantic notions and pretty pictures to discover a play obsessively concerned with psychology, metaphors and the absurdity of the human condition. In the cast were actors, all products of the Hall/Brook/Saint-Denis RSC, who would continue to make major contributions during the next decade and beyond: Alan Howard, Ben Kingsley, Sara Kestelman, Gemma Jones, Frances de la Tour, Patrick Stewart, John Kane, David Waller and Barry Stanton.[110] The RSC's most innovative treatment of a classic play proved to be its most popular: Brook's *Dream* travelled the world and stayed in the repertoire for four years.

Marat/Sade, 1964-66. Susan Williamson, Glenda Jackson, Ian Richardson. Production: Peter Brook. Design: Sally Jacobs. Photograph: Photo 12 / Alamy.

6   Defeating the Censor

Hall and Brook's campaign against censorship was at the heart of their radical agenda. In the 1960s the Lord Chamberlain was still enforcing the Theatre Act of 1843, which gave his office the power to ban the production of plays on the grounds of 'good manners', 'decorum' and 'public peace'. The rules forbade profanity, indecency, sedition and the representation of living persons. All new works had to be submitted before their presentation; the Lord Chamberlain could refuse a licence without consultation, but in practice was more likely to ask for specific changes. Theatre clubs could operate more freely.

Playwrights were unable to use four-letter words, or to explore, overtly, themes of sexuality; theatres were unable to satirise politicians or to criticise Britain's allies or to question organised religion. The RSC under Peter Hall, by taking things to the limit and beyond, was instrumental in ending a system of censorship that allowed a Court official, at that time a former governor of the Bank of England, to remove the word 'piss' from a contemporary play.

Hall initially staged work likely to offend the censor in theatre clubs – the season at the Arts in 1962 and Brook's *Theatre of Cruelty* project at LAMDA and the Donmar in 1964 (the Lord Chamberlain's letter objecting to Genet's *The Screens* was mockingly read out to the audience); but this changed later that year when he staged a challenging programme at the Aldwych, including David Rudkin's *Afore Night Come*, Roger Vitrac's *Victor* and Peter Weiss's *Marat/Sade*. Hall told the Lord Chamberlain that every cut would be printed in the programmes. The 1964 season outraged the Establishment and Hall's enemies, including the West End impresario and RSC governor Emile Littler who condemned the season as 'dirt' and a 'disgrace' in a letter to the *London Evening News*. The RSC viewed this attack as potentially very damaging since it gave ammunition to the supporters of censorship and the critics of state funding of the arts. Fordham Flower issued a statement supporting Hall, as did the directors and actors of the Company.[111] Next, the anti-Americanism of Brook's *US* worried the government. The Lord Chamberlain, Lord Cobald, invited Hall to St James's Palace late one night. The expectation was that a civilised man-to-man chat over drinks would be enough for Hall to do the 'right thing'. Was it right, Lord Cobald asked, to take money from the government with one hand while bashing its biggest ally with the other? Hall evoked freedom of speech and held his ground. Cobald sought to influence the RSC's Chairman, but Fordham Flower supported Brook and Hall. The cumulative effect of all this initiated a high-profile debate that resulted in the end of theatre censorship two years later.

7 John Barton

The origins of the Stratford revolution of the 1960s can be traced back to Peter Hall's student days at Cambridge. Cambridge theatre of the late 1940s and early 1950s owed much to John Barton, then a student at King's College but already a theatre man who combined scholarship with stagecraft (this most analytical examiner of texts was also a fight director). Barton remained a don-like figure, while his eccentricities provided anecdotes for generations of actors. Despite his training as a Shakespeare scholar, Barton was a fearless interpreter, prepared to adapt, cut and even write new dialogue if he felt it was needed. This resulted in a dubious version of Shakespeare's *King John* (1974). For Barton, the practical requirements of actors and the theatre were paramount.

Barton remained at King's (as fellow and Lay Dean) until 1960, when Peter Hall asked him to join the RSC. Hall wanted his friend's depth of knowledge as a Shakespearean scholar. Barton's unhappy experience directing Peter O'Toole and Peggy Ashcroft in *The Taming of the Shrew* led Hall to conclude that Barton would need time to learn how to direct professional actors. For the next four years his RSC work consisted of teaching, adaptations and co-direction (he was not a member of the directorate). Barton supported Hall by co-directing *Troilus and Cressida* in 1960 and by editing the three parts of *Henry VI* and *Richard III* to create the text of *The Wars of the Roses* trilogy in 1963. Hall directed the trilogy 'with' Barton and Frank Evans.

Barton returned to solo directing in 1965. Consistency of tone gave his productions an un-Shakespearean sense of pure logic. *Twelfth Night* (1969-72) is remembered with affection as a sublime romantic comedy imbued with melancholy. It is a mistake to view Barton as solely a text man: he employed considerable stagecraft – sounds of the sea, candlelight, painterly compositions – to achieve the beguiling atmosphere of his *Twelfth Night*. *Richard II* (1973-74) is the best example of Barton's method of interpreting a play, of taking an intellectual view and changing the text to make it work. Ian Richardson and Richard Pasco alternated the roles of Richard and Bolingbroke to emphasise their interchangeability as tragic figures. Barton's Bolingbroke was already Shakespeare's Henry IV, speaking the great lines on sleeplessness and the strain of kingship from the later play ('uneasy lies the head that wears the crown'). Barton also used stylised staging devices (the actors started the play in their rehearsal clothes; they frequently spoke directly to the audience) and a few symbolic objects, including a mirror, to make implicit the correlation between the king, forced to assume a role, and the actor playing him.

In the mid-1970s Barton returned to the comedies. *Much Ado About Nothing* (1976) was ingeniously set in India at the height of the British Raj. The social rules of military and colonial life fitted the play perfectly. Even more evocative was his melancholy version (set on bare boards beneath autumnal trees) of the early comedy *Love's Labour's Lost* (1978). In Barton's interpretation, the King of Navarre and his friends began the play as immature undergraduates; by its end each had been transformed by a much more knowing young woman. *Hamlet* (1980) used theatre as a metaphor (the platform stage was surrounded by all the props needed for the performance), but it was the least self-advertising of Barton's major productions, as rich, complex and thrilling as the text.

Also in 1980 Barton fulfilled a long-standing ambition by

staging at the Aldwych a cycle of Greek plays. He adapted the work of Euripides, Sophocles, Aeschylus and Homer into a single narrative telling the story of the Trojan War. Ten plays were performed over three evenings. As co-author he added his own scenes and freely changed the meaning of the texts to achieve a continuous narrative. After *The Greeks* Barton started to write an original play based on the myth of Tantalus, and during the twenty years he worked on the project he gradually became less active as a director. To stage *Tantalus* the RSC formed a partnership with the Denver Center for the Performing Arts. Peter Hall's production opened in 2000, but without its author who objected to Hall's changes and cuts. Given Barton's history as an adaptor and editor of playwrights' texts, his indignation provoked a certain irony. The rift was a reminder that the Hall/Barton axis had always been prone to volatility, with flare-ups occurring in 1960 (Hall demotes Barton at the RSC), 1973 (Hall moves to the National and poaches the RSC actress Susan Fleetwood) and 1978 (Barton's decision to stage *The Greeks* steals the thunder on Hall's planned production of *The Oresteia*).

Perhaps Barton's influence as a director of Shakespeare was closely aligned to his skill as a teacher, and therefore usefully summed up by the series of workshops he conducted with RSC actors for Channel Four in 1984 (*Playing Shakespeare*). They formed the basis of a book that is used by actors throughout the English-speaking world as a manual on the performing of Shakespeare. Barton's special ability to inspire actors through a process of forensic enquiry into how Shakespeare's language works, as revealed in *Playing Shakespeare*, is the reason why his productions are remembered for the quality of the ensemble playing: Judi Dench, Donald Sinden, Lisa Harrow and Emrys James in *Twelfth Night*; Pasco and Richardson in *Richard II*; Dench and Sinden in *Much Ado About Nothing*; Michael Pennington, Jane Lapotaire and Richard Griffiths in *Love's Labour's Lost*.

Barton remained influential. During a question and answer session in 2002, Dominic Cooke, director of an RSC production of John Marston's *The Malcontent*, was asked about the difficulty of interpreting this rarely performed 17th century text: he replied that John Barton had dropped by to tell the company the meaning of the words. This anecdote, however slight and amusing, seems to sum up the contribution of a director who devoted his entire career to one theatre company.

8 Handing Over

Hall's workload continued to be damaging to his personal life. His marriage to Leslie Caron ended in divorce.

1966 was a decisive year. The Arts Council refused to increase the RSC's grant and Hall responded with uncharacteristic negativity, mounting a cost-cutting season of revivals. For the first time he worked outside of the RSC, directing Mozart's *The Magic Flute* at the Royal Opera House. Most significantly, that summer Fordham Flower died. Hall faced a future working life dominated by the struggle for funding without Flower's support. Normally, for Hall, such frustrations were mitigated by a relish for the fight, but in 1967, missing Flower, suffering from shingles, feeling trapped and creatively restless, he was in a depressed state. He made a rash decision and resigned.[112] Because of Hall's confident public persona, both his vulnerability and his belief in collaboration were rarely acknowledged. If the creation of the RSC was only possible because of Hall's personal ambition and natural ability to play the political game at the same level as the Establishment grandees and apparatchiks who guarded access to the coffers, and it was, the scale of the Company's artistic achievements resulted from Hall's knack of being firmly in charge while sharing the direction of the theatre with colleagues whose standing was equal to his own.

Hall's final act as artistic director was one of his most inspired: he believed that the inexperienced Trevor Nunn was the right man to take over, and the board followed his recommendation. Hall's colleagues found it hard to believe that he was stepping down. Nunn said to Hall: 'I'll mind the shop. You're going to go away, you're going to do other things. But on the understanding that you're going to come back, I will look after your Company for you.'[113]

At the same time, Michel Saint-Denis retired and Peter Brook started to spend as much time in France as in England. After the premiere of *A Midsummer Night's Dream* he settled in Paris for good. Although Hall and Brook remained co-directors of the RSC, they were mostly absent. Hall staged a number of new plays at the Aldwych, including Edward Albee's *A Delicate Balance* (1969), Simon Gray's *Dutch Uncle* (1969) and Harold Pinter's *Old Times* (1971).

Hall would later come to regret his sudden decision to step down, confessing in his autobiography that he had felt homeless since leaving the RSC.[114]

9 Peter Hall's RSC: Some Representative Actors

The first actor approached by Peter Hall to join the RSC was Peggy Ashcroft. Ashcroft had been England's leading stage actress since the 1920s. She was the first modern actress. Her performances, when compared to those of her male colleagues, seemed uncontrived. While John Gielgud was in love with the grand poetic statement and Laurence Olivier with dressing-up, the artifice of performance, Peggy Ashcroft was spontaneous and intuitive. She had adopted Shakespeare's young heroines – Desdemona opposite Paul Robeson at the Savoy in 1930; Imogen, Rosalind, Portia, Perdita and Miranda at the Old Vic in 1932/33; and Juliet opposite Gielgud and Olivier at the New in 1935 – as if each one was an alternative version of herself. She was perennially youthful and forward-looking. At the age of fifty-three she embraced the radicalism of Peter Hall's RSC, eventually joining the artistic directorate and leading the Company for three decades.

Ashcroft's RSC performances, not only in Shakespeare but also in new plays by Harold Pinter, Edward Albee and Marguerite Duras, showed the extent of her ambition for the Company. In the first season, 1960, she played Kate opposite Peter O'Toole in *The Taming of the Shrew*, Paulina in *The Winter's Tale*, the title role in *The Duchess of Malfi* and Madame Ranevsky alongside Gielgud in

Michel Saint-Denis's *The Cherry Orchard*, a production that, given her history with these two men, must have had particular meaning for her. But it was *The Wars of the Roses* (1963/64) that confirmed the transforming energy of Peter Hall's new company, so complete was the elegant Ashcroft's embodiment of Shakespeare's savage Queen Margaret.

Donald Sinden played York, one of Margaret's victims. Here was another unexpected transformation, for Sinden had previously been best known as a light comedian in films and on the West End stage. As a young actor he had appeared at Stratford in supporting roles (1946/47) before winning a movie contract with Rank. Sinden spent the 1950s looking urbane in a uniform or a linen suit. Hall, though, admired Sinden's verse-speaking, and realised that the bellow and bluster of the previous era, if subtly updated, could have a powerful impact. Ashcroft's Margaret needed such an adversary. Sinden would go on to entertain and enlighten audiences in a wide spectrum of work. His Malvolio in John Barton's *Twelfth Night* was a masterpiece of physical invention and unforeseen vocal inflexions.

Another actor with traditional virtues was the intimidating Brewster Mason. Mason, an ex-Navy man, had a commanding presence and a voice to match. In the wings during a 1967 RSC performance of *Coriolanus*, he lifted Helen Mirren off the ground by the neck for corpsing.[115] Mason was a student at RADA when the war claimed him. His acting career began at the end of the 1940s. He played Polixenes to John Gielgud's Leontes in Peter Brook's *The Winter's Tale* in the West End. Gielgud was an important influence, directing Mason in supporting roles in a number of plays, including *Richard II* at Stratford (1952). At the RSC, Mason gave richly detailed if classically orthodox performances in all genres. He was Kent in *King Lear*, Warwick in *The Wars of the Roses* and Claudius in *Hamlet*, but also Sir Toby Belch in *Twelfth Night* and Goldberg in Harold Pinter's *The Birthday Party*. For Terry Hands, during the 1970s, Mason would play Falstaff in the two parts of *Henry IV* and *The Merry Wives of Windsor*.

Ian Holm made his name at Stratford during the 1950s. By the time Peter Hall took charge of the theatre, Holm was ready to lead a generational change in the acting of Shakespeare. His performances as Richard of Gloucester/Richard III and as the first non-heroic Hal/Henry V in the 1963/64 history cycle, classical in technique but contemporary in style, helped to define Hall's RSC. Holm's versatility as a Shakespearean meant that he could master any character, from Troilus to Ariel, from Malvolio to Romeo. In 1965 Holm created the role of Lenny, the pimp, in Harold Pinter's *The Homecoming*. Some writers creep into an actor's psyche and Holm can claim both Shakespeare and Pinter. As imagined by Holm, Richard III and Lenny, Lear and Max, merged into one another across the centuries.

Eric Porter was only in his thirties when he responded to Hall's call in 1960, but he had an older man's authority, capable of a stern and forbidding demeanour that lent itself to rulers and churchmen. Ulysses in *Troilus and Cressida*, the title role in Jean Anouilh's *Becket*, Macbeth, and Bolingbroke in *Richard II* were formidably presented. He also played strong men in decline or crisis – Leontes in *The Winter's Tale*, Henry IV (the continuation of Bolingbroke, played in the same season), the title role in *Doctor Faustus* – and Malvolio in *Twelfth Night*.

Derek Godfrey has almost faded from the theatrical record. Today it is difficult to find an obituary, let alone a full account of his life and work. And yet Godfrey was a pivotal RSC member during the early Hall years, memorable as Orsino in *Twelfth Night*, Hector in *Troilus and Cressida*, Antonio in *The Duchess of Malfi*, Petruchio, and Macheath in *The Beggar's Opera*. Godfrey returned to the RSC in 1971, and again at the beginning of the 1980s to play Jaques in *As You Like It* and Buckingham in *Richard III* for Terry Hands, and Claudius in *Hamlet* for John Barton. This phase of work was cut short by his death in 1983.

Richard Johnson and Dorothy Tutin were already Stratford, and national, stars. They had appeared together in Jean Anouilh's *The Lark* in the West End, and were a glamorous Romeo and Juliet at Stratford in 1958. They were stolen away by the movies, but returned to Stratford for Hall's first seasons. The versatile Johnson played Aguecheek in *Twelfth Night* and Grandier in John Whiting's *The Devils*. He would later lead Trevor Nunn's *The Romans* company as Mark Antony in *Julius Caesar* and *Antony and Cleopatra*. Dorothy Tutin was Sister Jeanne in *The Devils*, Portia, Viola in *Twelfth Night*, Cressida, Varya in *The Cherry Orchard*, and Rosalind.

A twenty-year-old actress called Diana Rigg, new to Stratford, turned heads walking-on in unnamed parts during the 1959 season. Peter Hall knew that he had discovered a pretty ingénue, but one with the talent to become an important classical actress. He offered her one of the new RSC contracts and cast her as Andromache in *Troilus and Cressida*, Gwendolen in Anouilh's *Becket*, Bianca in *The Taming of the Shrew*, Helena in *A Midsummer Night's Dream* and Adriana in *The Comedy of Errors*. For Peter Brook, she played Cordelia in *King Lear* and Monika Stettler in *The Physicists*. By her middle twenties she was one of the RSC's brightest players, and it was a stroke of inspiration by the makers of *The Avengers* to cast this elegant classical actress as the action heroine Emma Peel. She returned to the RSC in 1966 to play Viola in *Twelfth Night*, and then took up the opportunities in movies created by the success of *The Avengers*.

Hall was eager to bring in the best younger actors and to cast them in leading roles. The most eccentric of these emerging stars was David Warner. Warner was very tall, had a mop of fair hair and wore glasses. He was far from being a stereotypical leading actor, but Hall, impressed by his originality and ability to command a stage, cast him as Henry VI and Richard II in the history cycle. Hall's choice of the unconventional Warner to star in his revival of *Hamlet* was a masterstroke. The production became an event, with queues for returns and crowds of young people waiting at the stage door. Warner's Hamlet was an undergraduate in a long red scarf – lanky and awkward with an acute sense of irony (when he put on a crown it dropped over his eyes). Disaffected, classless and anti-establishment, he spoke directly to young theatregoers and achieved pop star status during the two-year run.

As the daughter of Michael Redgrave, Vanessa Redgrave was already famous when she joined the RSC. Her performance as Rosalind in 1962 was received with rapture, an absolute rarity; she was suddenly the most feted actress of a remarkable generation. She stayed with the RSC only for another year, playing Imogen in *Cymbeline* for William Gaskill, before embarking on a film career. David Warner and Vanessa Redgrave starred opposite each other in Karel Reisz's *Morgan, a Suitable Case for Treatment* (1966).

Another important discovery was an actor from Edinburgh who would be a vital figure at the RSC for the next fifteen years, Ian Richardson. Few actors have played as many classical roles; fewer still with such precision and style, for Richardson was easily the most imperious (and chilling) actor of his generation. The crystal clarity of his voice and the sheer inventiveness of his imagination linked his performances as Antipholus of Ephesus in *The Comedy of Errors*, the Herald in *Marat/Sade*, Vindice in *The Revenger's Tragedy*, Ford in *The Merry Wives of Windsor*, Pericles, Berowne in *Love's Labour's Lost*, and Richard III. His collaboration with John Barton, between 1967 and 73, was particularly productive – Coriolanus, Cassius, Prospero, Angelo in *Measure for Measure* and both Richard and Bolingbroke, alternated with Richard Pasco, in the renowned *Richard II*.

A young actress called Glenda Jackson stood out among the novice performers assembled by Peter Brook to work on the *Theatre of Cruelty* project. With her intelligent eyes, tousled fringe and high cheekbones, she looked more like a student activist than a young actress. She made a lasting impression as the mad girl playing Charlotte Corday in Peter Weiss's *Marat/Sade*, and was the leading actress in the rehearsed reading of Weiss's *The Investigation* and the protest piece *US*. The intention of Brook's programme was that it should influence the RSC's mainstream work. Glenda Jackson was also cast in classical roles, including the Princess of France in *Love's Labour's Lost* and Ophelia in the David Warner *Hamlet*. Years later, reunited with Brook, she would play an abrasive, volatile, unromantic Cleopatra to Alan Howard's Antony in *Antony and Cleopatra*.

Two young actresses from South Africa, Janet Suzman and Estelle Kohler, joined the Company at around the same time. Janet Suzman made an immediate impact as Joan of Arc in *The Wars of the Roses*. Projecting a strong image of integrity and intelligence she claimed many of Shakespeare's heroines (stressing their independent spirit and courage) in a ten-year journey that took her from the early comedies to the late tragedies: Luciana in *The Comedy of Errors*, Lady Anne in *Richard III*, Rosaline, Portia, Timandra in *Timon of Athens*, Kate in *The Taming of the Shrew*, Beatrice opposite Alan Howard, and Rosalind. She would later, for Trevor Nunn, play Cleopatra and Lavinia in *Titus Andronicus*.

Estelle Kohler succeeded Glenda Jackson as Ophelia and went on to give admired performances as Olivia in *Twelfth Night*, Lady Percy in the first part of *Henry IV*, Virgilia in *Coriolanus*, Helena in *All's Well That Ends Well*, Juliet to Ian Holm's Romeo, Isabella in *Measure for Measure*, Sylvia in *The Two Gentlemen of Verona* and Miranda in *The Tempest*. She would remain a member of the Company under Trevor Nunn, Terry Hands and Adrian Noble.

Among Hall's other significant players, either established or emerging, were Paul Rogers (Falstaff, Max in Harold Pinter's *The Homecoming*), Peter McEnery (Silvius in *As You Like It*, Johnny in David Rudkin's *Afore Night Come*), and Charles Thomas (Berowne, Mark Antony, Orsino in *Twelfth Night*). Charles Thomas was on the point of stardom when he died tragically of an overdose of prescription pills during the RSC's 1970 tour of Australia.

The actor Hall wanted in the RSC more than any other was the elusive Paul Scofield. The leading classical actor of the post-war generation, Scofield had become a star without ever chasing fame. His career was inextricably linked to that of Peter Brook. They had emerged together working for Barry Jackson first at the Birmingham Rep and then at Stratford, where Scofield played Don Armado in *Love's Labour's Lost* and Mercutio in *Romeo and Juliet* (1946/47). Scofield caused as big a stir (and wounded as many hearts) playing the Young Shepherd in *The Winter's Tale* as the title role in *Hamlet*. If his physical presence appealed to everyone, his mannered vocal style divided opinion. However, as much as anything, it was the range of his voice that allowed him to play older men and to alternate romantic leads with sardonic character parts. Brook and Scofield's partnership continued with a season at the Phoenix Theatre consisting of *Hamlet*, Graham Greene's *The Power and the Glory* and T.S. Eliot's *The Family Reunion* (1955). The anguish and melancholy, power and subtlety, nobility and stoicism of Scofield's Hamlet moved and excited a generation of theatregoers.

Scofield's sudden withdrawal from the RSC on the eve of the 1960 season caused a crisis, but Hall didn't take it personally. Two years later Hall tried again with an offer of King Lear directed by

Brook. With contracts signed Scofield sent a doctor's note. Instead of cancelling Hall postponed *King Lear* until the autumn. Scofield's devastating and devastated Lear was worth waiting for. He stayed at the RSC until 1967, playing Timon of Athens, Khlestakov in Gogol's *The Government Inspector* and, for Hall, Macbeth, after which he suddenly quit, never to return.

Below: *A Midsummer Night's Dream* by Shakespeare. An RSC film, 1967. David Warner (Lysander), Helen Mirren (Hermia), Ian Holm (Puck). Directed by Peter Hall. Photograph: Everett Collection / Alamy. Opposite: Helen Mirren in 1968. Photograph by Neil Libbert / Bridgeman Images.

The Island of the Mighty by John Arden, Aldwych, 1972. Estelle Kohler (Gwenhwyvar) and Patrick Allen (Arthur) in rehearsal. Production: David Jones. Design: Tazeena Firth. Photograph: *Evening Standard* / Hulton Archive, Getty Images.

4

Trevor Nunn and Terry Hands

A Midsummer Night's Dream by Shakespeare, RST, 1970. Production: Peter Brook. Design: Sally Jacobs. Photograph by Donald Cooper / Alamy.

Top, l-r: Mary Rutherford (Hermia), Christopher Gable (Lysander), Frances de la Tour (Helena), Ben Kingsley (Demetrius); bottom, l-r: John Kane (Puck), David Waller (Bottom), Sara Kestelman (Titania), Alan Howard (Oberon).

1 Transition

Trevor Nunn followed in Peter Hall's footsteps before making his own way as an innovative producer. He took his mentor's model and expanded it in new directions.

His task at the beginning was daunting. Although Nunn had been chosen by Hall, he was only twenty-eight and his appointment was met with considerable scepticism. He had come to the RSC with an impressive record from Cambridge (he had taken student productions to the Edinburgh Festival)[116] and the Belgrade Theatre, Coventry (1962-65), but his first solo RSC assignments – *The Thwarting of Baron Bolligrew* and *Tango* – were failures. It was said that he lacked authority in the rehearsal room.[117]

Nunn turned things around with his next project, the Jacobean rarity *The Revenger's Tragedy*. The production opened during the crisis year of 1966, after the Arts Council had frozen the RSC's grant, leading *The Observer*'s Ronald Bryden to write: 'Every time the Arts Council tightens its screws on the Company's subsidy, arguing that one National Theatre is enough, the RSC bounces back with some victory of sheer theatrical resource over economics, so brilliant as to suggest it works best with its back against the wall.'[118] Since 1960 the RSC's main stage had been the domain of an austere style of Brechtian realism, the mode favoured by Peter Hall, John Barton and John Bury. *The Revenger's Tragedy* was the work of artists new to the Company – Nunn, the designer Christopher Morley (Nunn and Morley had previously worked together at the Belgrade) and the actors Alan Howard, Norman Rodway and John Kane. It seemed like a deliberate departure – stylised and overtly theatrical, a macabre carnival in black and silver. Bryden continued: 'Balancing terror and absurdity, it points way back to a kind of theatrical response killed off by naturalism and the novel. [...] The masked court whirls in a torchlit pavane out of a sable limbo into diseased phosphorescence.'[119] The fact that *The Revenger's Tragedy* was a Jacobean thriller, the first to be performed on a stage usually reserved for Shakespeare, partly explained its impact. Hall approved Nunn's vision in the face of opposition from Barton and others. It turned out, though, to be just one of a number of different styles adopted by the young director. He was, at heart, closer to Hall than to his friend and contemporary Terry Hands. It was Hands, and not Nunn, who took the lessons of *The Revenger's Tragedy* forward.

In the next year Nunn confirmed his new status with assured productions of *The Taming of the Shrew*, starring Janet Suzman (whom he later married) and Michael Williams, and *The Relapse*. His elevation divided the RSC along generational lines (although Peggy Ashcroft took to Nunn as she had taken to Hall a decade before). A few years later Nunn would write:

> When I had to follow Peter Hall, at thrilling and daunting short notice, I had just about learned how to run a rehearsal; I hadn't a clue about running anything bigger. I had only ever used somebody else's secretary to type the odd letter, I had never chaired a meeting, I couldn't read a balance sheet, and I was totally unaccustomed to public speaking – so I made no prophetic pronouncements. Continuity was the word.[120]

Hall continued as a co-director of the Company, alongside Nunn, Brook and Peggy Ashcroft, and the RSC talked about a change of roles rather than a new beginning.

Nunn, supported by his chief associates Terry Hands, John Barton and David Jones, quickly silenced his critics. Hall's practical arrangements had been based around three-year blocks of work, during which the actors would, ideally, play in both Stratford and London during the same year. Nunn realised that this system was no longer working effectively: too many actors were only working for two years and taking one year 'out'. Nunn's arrangement was based around two-year cycles, year one in Stratford, year two in

London. He believed that the Company had become too large and that its actors were doing too much 'less well than they were able'. He reconfirmed the importance of permanence and put his faith in a smaller nucleus of players who, alongside leading characters, would play supporting and minor parts. Looking back on his first five years in 1974, he wrote:

> The RSC must be the most expert, skilled and distinctive troupe performing the plays of Shakespeare in the world. We *can* be at present, but randomly. The necessary skills can only be achieved with permanence. But the ensemble can only work if there is *one* group, and if there are no hierarchic distinctions within the group.[121]

The new system meant that successful productions could stay in the repertoire for longer, but placed an extra burden on the players, asked to play three or four parts at any one time. At the same time, Nunn reconfirmed one of Hall's key ideas, the cross-fertilisation of the classic and the new, but with no illusion as to the challenge its realisation presented. Although he intended for the Company to spend fifty per cent of its time performing plays other than Shakespeare, finding important new plays – especially plays big enough to succeed on the main stage – was a continual challenge. The heady days of the 1960s, when Hall first worked with Harold Pinter and discovered John Whiting and David Rudkin, and when Peter Brook was staging radical new work, were not repeatable. Nunn looked for works with multiple roles that would benefit from the skills of a classical troupe performing in a large theatre, plays that explored the human condition, but had to accept that most plays that came across his desk, however fine and important they might be, were written for small casts and were narrowly political in scope: they were clearly better suited to the Royal Court. However, there were notable exceptions. Nunn and Hands mounted main house productions of new plays by Tom Stoppard (*Travesties* in 1974 and *Every Good Boy Deserves Favour* in 1977), David Mercer (*After Haggerty* in 1970 and *Duck Song* in 1974), Peter Barnes (*The Bewitched* in 1974 and *Red Noses* in 1985), John Arden (*The Island of the Mighty* in 1972), Peter Nichols (*Passion Play* in 1981 and *Poppy* in 1982), and David Edgar (*Nicholas Nickleby* in 1980 and *Maydays* in 1983). There were some notable flops too. Once Nunn opened the studio theatres, he was able to increase the number of new works presented by the Company (see the chapter on small-scale work).

Nunn's first season (1969) felt like a departure: a new stage configuration was designed by Christopher Morley (a white box that placed emphasis on space, colour and light) and the choice of plays was the most challenging in years: three of Shakespeare's late plays, a mature comedy and a play by one of Shakespeare's contemporaries. Nunn directed *The Winter's Tale* and *Henry VIII*, Hands *Pericles* and Middleton's *Women Beware Women*, and Barton *Twelfth Night*. The leading roles were played by Judi Dench (wonderfully expressive and engaging as Viola and Hermione), Donald Sinden (gloriously comic as Malvolio), Richard Pasco, Emrys James, Charles Thomas, Lisa Harrow, Brewster Mason, Brenda Bruce, Roger Rees and Jeffery Dench. The season was a critical and popular success (the RSC's audience grew during Nunn's first years). Nunn introduced more international touring: this filled the gap between Stratford and London (the Stratford season ended in November until 1974, when Nunn extended it into the New Year); it was also financially profitable. All of Nunn's early changes were made in the context of the RSC's precarious financial state – his choices were both creative and fiscally cunning. The integrated approach and box set style of 1969 remained influential.

Nevertheless, it took several years for Nunn's directorship to fully come into its own. First, he had to negotiate his way through a phase of uncertainty and stress.

The Two Gentlemen of Verona by Shakespeare, RST, 1970. Helen Mirren in rehearsal.
Photograph by Donald Cooper / Alamy.

The Two Gentlemen of Verona by Shakespeare, RST, 1970. Estelle Kohler (Silvia), Helen Mirren (Julia). Production: Robin Phillips. Design: Daphne Dare. Photograph by Donald Cooper / Alamy.

2 National Theatres

In April 1972 Peter Hall told his RSC colleagues that he was leaving to run the National Theatre. The break was hard for Hall, Nunn, David Brierley, Peter Brook and Peggy Ashcroft and led to a shared fantasy that the National and the RSC could merge. That July, over lunch, they discussed the idea in earnest. Hall wrote in his diary:

> My proposition is that the RSC should leave the Aldwych and run the NT's proscenium theatre, the Lyttelton, on the South Bank as the first step in a fusion. Then, when the RSC moves into the Barbican, it would offer continuous major Shakespeare productions and there would be no Shakespeare on the South Bank. This was an idea I had already sketched out with David Brierley and with Trevor. But it was encouraging now to find Peter Brook also thinking of it as the only sensible rationalization.[122]

Not only did these RSC colleagues think that there wouldn't be enough resources for the two companies to operate separately in London once the South Bank theatre opened; they wanted to keep their 'family' together. It is revealing that the others looked upon Hall, younger than Brook by five years, as the leader of their group, something that Hall found had disadvantages as well as advantages, for it was no doubt taken for granted that he would pay the expensive lunch bill. Following a restaurant dinner with Brook and Nunn in 1979, Hall wrote: 'Who paid for dinner, all fifty quids' worth? I did of course. That must stop.'[123]

Hall alerted Arnold Goodman, the outgoing chairman of the Arts Council, to the amalgamation idea. Goodman gave his enthusiastic support. His secretary-general, Hugh Willatt, was less convinced. He had always argued for the independence of the RSC and the NT, believing that the existence of two great competing theatres benefitted the British theatre as a whole. Hall's point, shared by Nunn, was that the opening of the South Bank complex would, inevitably, change the nature of the RSC's role in London. Patrick Gibson, Goodman's successor, was prepared to keep an open mind. Interestingly, the RSC's core governors, when told of the idea by their chairman, George Farmer, were sceptical, believing Hall to be at his 'old empire-building tactics'.[124]

Hall knew that Laurence Olivier, still the NT's director during the interim period before he formally took over, would need to be carefully managed. Back in the early 1960s, when the RSC was being created in the face of the NT movement, Hall and Olivier hadn't been able to find a way of merging their companies despite pressure from the Arts Council to do so. Both sides feared being subsumed by the other, and the difference in aesthetics between Hall's conception of a national theatre and Olivier's was also a factor. It mirrored the differences between the two men. Hall was a Cambridge intellectual, a director in the modern sense, ideas-driven and holistic; Olivier was the biggest star actor of the age, and by temperament an actor-manager of the old school. This problem no longer applied, for, intellectually, Hall's NT was not going to be in opposition to Nunn's RSC. Although Olivier was on the way out, he wielded power and was Machiavellian by instinct. Hall was Machiavellian by design.

Olivier initially indicated that he thought the merger was a good idea. Within days, though, he was backtracking, displeased by Hall's predictable assertion that Nunn should be his second-in-command after the merger. Olivier thought that one of his lieutenants, Michael Blakemore, should be given this role; if not, the merger would look like a Stratford takeover. But for Hall, this was non-negotiable. At a meeting of the core participants – Hall, Olivier, Nunn, George Farmer and Patrick Donnell[125] – called and chaired by Arnold Goodman, Olivier didn't attempt to derail the merger, but indicated that it shouldn't be guaranteed that Nunn would assume the top position should Hall be 'run over by a bus'. George Farmer, for the RSC, was as wary as Olivier, asking Hall why, if he believed that there might be insufficient money and talent to maintain two large companies (Hall, making the case for the merger, had just said this), he had persuaded Stratford's board to form the RSC and move into London back in 1960/61? Hall could only come up with the weak response that 'times have changed'.

Part of the problem was that Olivier was conflicted in his own mind and couldn't bring himself to declare wholehearted support for either independence or merger. The psychology was complex. He couldn't bear the thought of Stratford taking over the National Theatre, but a part of him didn't want any of his own people to inherit his crown.

At the beginning of 1973 Hall and Nunn drafted a paper in support of the merger. Hall took it to Olivier and said that he had signed it but that Nunn would sign it too as he had done most of the work. Olivier fell into Hall's trap and immediately said that he would sign it also. A few days later, on the way with Hall to attend the next meeting of the two sides with Goodman, Olivier said that he now regretted signing the paper. At the meeting he explained that he wanted to withdraw his name and George Farmer 'solemnly took out his Biro and crossed his name out'.[126] It was not a bad outcome for Hall and Nunn.

However, problems arose between the two friends. Hall wanted the RSC's outstanding press officer John Goodwin to join him at the NT straight away. Nunn and Brierley baulked at this. Hall's capture of Goodwin suggested that he had started to plan for the merger not happening. His diary entry for 29 March 1973 reveals that he was having second thoughts, but also that Nunn's commitment was wavering (although this may have been Hall's way of justifying his own doubts):

> I find myself getting more and more worried about the NT/RSC merger. Will Trevor push it enough? And will it happen in time to support all the important work we at the National have to do in the next eighteen months in order to get the building open? Also, now I am getting to grips with the needs of the South Bank, I am appalled by the size of that operation alone.[127]

Only a week later, Hall met Goodman by chance at Liverpool Station. Goodman was still in favour of a merger, but felt that without Olivier's unequivocal public support the 'political difficulties were extreme'.[128] He advised Hall to abandon it. Again, by giving Goodman a prominent position, Hall may have been trying to justify an awkward decision (easily interpreted as a betrayal of his old RSC friends) that he was preparing to take himself.

Hall was right in wanting to resolve the matter one way or the other. Without telling Nunn, he leaked the merger idea to *The Daily Telegraph* in an attempt to polarise views. As he predicted, and hoped, the public reaction was mostly hostile. Olivier's NT associates, learning of the scheme for the first time, were understandably bitter. Hall still found it difficult to tell Nunn that he had changed his mind about the merger. Instead, he came up with the idea of an association of the two companies that would allow them to share the South Bank building until the RSC moved to the Barbican. The RSC would deliver all of the Shakespeare productions on the South Bank. NT actors would be available to be cast in RSC productions, and Hall and Nunn would sit on both boards. The managements would merge, but the companies would continue as separate entities. A full merger could easily happen later on, if wanted. Nunn wasn't convinced, not least because the RSC would be restricted to performing only Shakespeare in London: he still wanted the full merger, and as soon as possible. Olivier was enthusiastic, then unenthusiastic: his usual pattern. He didn't want the RSC to be given any more than two months of the year on the South Bank.

At any rate, Hall was simply working things through in his own mind until he could justify a conclusion he had wanted for some time. On 8 August he wrote in his diary:

> The merger now seems to me one of the silliest ideas I have ever been seduced by. The reasons I once wanted it are obvious – it would have been wonderful to work again with my old RSC colleagues, and it would have saved them and the NT from our present money difficulties. But the size of the resulting organization would have induced artistic paralysis.[129]

In the end it was Hall, and not Olivier or anyone else, who killed the merger. In September 1973 he finally told Nunn and Brierley that he didn't believe that the merger was achievable. They reluctantly agreed. Hall and Nunn would lobby the Arts Council for adequate funding for both theatres.

It was the right decision. Nunn, in particular, had been motivated by a combination of emotion and fear. He had yet to feel comfortable handling the pressure of running the RSC. He was wrong in thinking that his company wouldn't prosper when forced into competition with a mighty NT on the South Bank, and he couldn't have known how close he was to coming into his own as the leader of the RSC. He needed to break his dependency on Hall; to accept that there would be some creative advantages in having to function with less money than the NT, and to rejoice in the fact that his company owned itself and was independent of the state. The rejection of the merger idea turned out to be, for Nunn, a necessary process, a rite of passage.

As for Hall, his advocacy of the merger blatantly contradicted the arguments he had used when creating and defending the RSC back in the 1960s, and seemed to indicate that he was emotionally conflicted over his decision to leave the RSC for the National: it was as if he needed to go through this process before he could commit completely to his new theatre. Now that this had been achieved, he acted ruthlessly in the interests of the National. The following episode indicates the strain that Hall, Barton and Nunn were under. Hall offered Susan Fleetwood, then with the RSC, a part in a forthcoming NT production (her agent said she would be free). He received accusatory telegrams from Nunn ('Shocked and upset that my leading lady has been approached by you with no contact between us') and Barton ('Am not surprised at how you go at it as always thought you would but am wryly disgusted at how soon and crudely you set about it. There are still telephones and I thought manners').[130] Hall and Nunn made peace a couple of weeks later, but battle lines had been drawn.

Nunn had to deal with the consequences of Hall's departure just as the demands of running the RSC were beginning to catch up on him. He was exhausted from staging the four plays of *The Romans* at Stratford; then his comment in a letter to *The Times* that the RSC was 'a basically left-wing organisation' caused a furore.[131] Nunn was responding to accusations by John Arden and Margaretta D'Arcy that the RSC was deliberately turning their Arthurian play *The Island of the Mighty* – David Jones directed Estelle Kohler, Patrick Allen and Emrys James at the Aldwych – into a defence of imperialism. Angus Maude, the Tory MP for Stratford, resigned as an RSC governor as a result of the comment; George Farmer said that the RSC was not a left-wing organisation in the political sense, but defended Nunn (*The Times*, 7 December 1972); David Hare called, along with other writers, for the creation of a playwrights' union to defend their rights against perfidious theatre managements (*The Times*, 7 December 1972).

The controversy passed, and Nunn came through his moment of crisis. His fears proved unfounded, for the RSC of 1975 to 1982 eclipsed Hall's troubled NT.

Cyrano de Bergerac by Rostand, Barbican, 1983. Pete Postlethwaite, Alice Krige, Derek Jacobi, John Bowe. Production: Terry Hands. Design: Koltai. Photograph by Donald Cooper / Alamy.

Romeo and Juliet by Shakespeare, RST, 1976. Ian McKellen (Romeo). Production: Trevor Nunn. Design: John Napier. Photograph by Donald Cooper / Alamy.

The Other Place Theatre, Stratford. Photograph: unknown.

3 The Importance of Small-scale Work

Nunn believed in continuity but was restlessly creative. In the early 1970s he began the process that led to the opening of a studio theatre in Stratford.

Small-scale and experimental work had always been important to the RSC, but, with the exception of Peter Brook's *Theatre of Cruelty* season at LAMDA in 1964 and Michel Saint-Denis's workshop studio in Stratford (influential internally in terms of the training and development of actors), it had been additional to the Company's main operation. Because of limited funds, important seasons of small-scale work in London at the Arts Theatre Club in 1962 (Hall had wanted to acquire the Mercury Theatre in Notting Hill) and at The Place in 1971, 1973 and 1974 had not been sustainable.

The RSC's small-scale touring outfit, Theatregoround, established by Peter Hall in 1965, was supported by a grant from the Gulbenkian Foundation. It had its beginnings in a tour of social clubs and canteens undertaken by a group of four RSC actors funded by the RSC Club and called Actors Commando. Their thirty-minute lunchtime or early evening show consisted of extracts from Shakespeare and contemporary plays. By the end of the year Hall had made this outreach programme an official part of the Company. The unit, initially under Michael Kustow, created productions with small casts and rudimentary scenery, and visited schools, colleges and community centres in London and the Midlands (and later throughout the UK). The actors, mostly juniors within the RSC, worked on a voluntary basis. The aim was to reach new audiences, particularly young people from working-class backgrounds. TGR's pioneering spirit, combining theatre with educational workshops, was highly influential. Alongside John Barton's *The Battle of Agincourt*, a didactic adaptation of Shakespeare's *Henry V*, the early repertoire featured rarely performed short plays by major writers, including Chekhov's *The Proposal*, Dylan Thomas's *Under Milk Wood* and Harold Pinter's *The Dumb Waiter*, directed by Terry Hands, who ran TGR from 1966.

In 1970 the RSC mounted a Theatregoround Festival at the Roundhouse. Peter Brook's *A Midsummer Night's Dream*, Trevor Nunn's *Hamlet* and Terry Hands's *Richard III* were performed without décor or costumes. The RSC saw the potential of producing major productions of Shakespeare in a small space, where the actors could speak directly and intimately to spectators and where the poetic power of the words would be undiminished.[132] Instead of continuing with Theatregoround (its operation had become too costly), Nunn decided to convert Michel Saint-Denis's former studio in Southern Lane, a prefabricated tin hut erected without any intention of permanence back in 1964 and at that time used as the headquarters of Theatregoround, into a performance space.

In 1973 the RSC tried out the Studio, as it was still called, by mounting a limited season of four plays. Sensing the special quality of this inauspicious venue, Nunn invited the Company's youngest director, Buzz Goodbody, to formulate a policy and a programme for the theatre she named the Other Place. The name came from *Hamlet*, act 4, scene 3:

> CLAUDIUS: Where is Polonius? HAMLET: In heaven. Send hither to see. If your messenger find him not there, seek him i' th'other place yourself.

Together with Jean Moore (administrator) and Jill Frazier (stage manager), Goodbody did much of the painting and other preparation work. Except for two dressing rooms there was no backstage; there was no stage door; no bar. The Other Place offered a very austere and uncomfortable environment, but the close proximity of actors and spectators heightened the excitement of both performing and watching theatre. From the start the Other Place was looked upon as the Stratford company's second theatre rather than as a fringe venue, although Goodbody ensured that it had a particular role by forming new links with the local community and schools, and by offering an experience that was affordable, unstuffy and excitingly unpredictable.

During her first season in charge (1974) she directed *King Lear*, with Tony Church, Mike Gwilym and David Suchet. There were also productions by Howard Davies, Ron Daniels (*Afore Night Come*) and Nicol Williamson (*Uncle Vanya*). She planned a second season of *Hamlet*, Ben Jonson's *Epicene* and Brecht's *Man is Man*. *Hamlet*, which opened the season in April 1975, was a landmark. Staged with economy on a white set, it was performed in modern dress with conversational intensity by Ben Kingsley, George Baker, Mikel Lambert, Yvonne Nicholson, Bob Peck, Stuart Wilson and Griffith Jones.

Four days after the first preview, Buzz Goodbody committed suicide in her London flat. Two empty pill bottles and a note declaring that she intended to kill herself by overdosing on sleeping tablets were found in the room.[133] Trevor Nunn took over the Other Place season, and transferred *Hamlet* to London. He later entrusted the Other Place to Ron Daniels.

The Other Place would become the RSC's main theatre for new plays and rare classics, but its initial importance was in giving new life to the Company's performance of Shakespeare. Goodbody's *Hamlet* and Nunn's *Macbeth* (1976), with Ian McKellen, established the view, still widely held in England, that Shakespeare's plays are most powerfully presented as studies in character psychology rather than as narratives of action and spectacle.

The case for a second theatre had been won, and Nunn looked for a sister venue in London, eventually selecting the Donmar Warehouse[134] in Covent Garden and entrusting its operation (as a space for radical new work as well as TOP transfers) to Howard Davies (1977). Daniels and Davies spearheaded the RSC's new writing work for the next decade. There was no obvious division in quality between the new plays and the classics that played side by side. Daniels's productions of David Edgar's *Destiny* (1976), Stephen Poliakoff's *Breaking the Silence* (1984), Ford's *Tis Pity She's a Whore* (1977) and Shakespeare's *Pericles* (1979) were lucid and gripping – new plays staged as classics, classics staged as new plays. In particular, he advocated the work of David Rudkin, directing productions of *Afore Night Come* (1974), *The Sons of Light* (1977), *Hippolytus*, after Euripides (1978), and *Hansel and Gretel* (1980). At the Warehouse, Davies supported the writer, served the text and never self-advertised. As well as remaining doggedly faithful to those difficult masters Bond and Barker by directing revivals of *Bingo* (1976) and *The Fool* (1980) and the premieres of *The Bundle* (1977) and *The Loud Boy's Life* (1980), he fashioned hits from two quality middlebrow entertainments – Pam Gems's *Piaf* (1978) and C.P. Taylor's *Good* (1981). Among the other important plays premiered by the RSC in the studios were: Peter Whelan's *The Accrington Pals* in 1981; Peter Flannery's *Our Friends in the North* in 1982; Ron Hutchinson's *The Dillen* in 1983; Robert Holman's *Today* in 1984; Nicholas Wright's *The Desert Air* in 1984; Christopher Hampton's *Les Liaisons dangereuses* in 1985; and Nick Dear's *The Art of Success* in 1986.

Nunn further re-invigorated the RSC by establishing the annual Newcastle residency (1977)[135] and small-scale tour (1978). These important innovations made the RSC far more of a national theatre than the official NT in London. The small-scale tour was organised more or less annually until the end of Adrian Noble's tenure. Travelling with a mobile theatre enabled the RSC to perform in schools, leisure centres and church halls in areas poorly served by conventional theatres. The first troupe was led by Ian McKellen, Roger Rees, Bob Peck and Griffith Jones. They toured three plays – Nunn's *Three Sisters*, *Twelfth Night* and an anthology show called *And is There Honey Still for Tea?* The mobile theatre would later become more advanced; in 1978 it consisted only of a platform and a lighting rig.

The 1976 Stratford season was the high watermark of Nunn's RSC. Alongside the studio production of *Macbeth*, there were plays by Edward Bond, Bertolt Brecht and David Edgar (*Destiny*) and noteworthy main house revivals of *King Lear, Romeo and Juliet, Much Ado About Nothing* and *The Comedy of Errors*, and the players – Judi Dench, Ian McKellen, Donald Sinden, Michael Pennington, Roger Rees, Bob Peck, Michael Williams, Mike Gwilym, Tony Church, Patrick Stewart, David Waller, Ian McDiarmid, John Woodvine, David Waller, Griffith Jones, Francesca Annis, Barbara Leigh-Hunt, John Nettles and others – were among those talented and committed long-term RSC artists whose constant presence gave the RSC its strength in depth.

Of particular importance, Nunn brought on a new generation of directors and designers. He had realised at the very start of his directorship that Hall's decision to create an in-house team of co-directors had been vital and would continue to be so; but he saw the need to go further. Brook and Saint-Denis were enormously influential, but they rarely involved themselves in the day-to-day details of management, and, as directors, worked on their own special projects. Looking back, in 1997, Nunn explained that

> If you have a genuine ensemble company that wants to renew itself on an annual basis then there must be a group of directors who have previously dedicated themselves to working with that company. If you do not have a committed directorate and things are done in an ad hoc way, you run into trouble. For example, people who arrive to direct a single play and who are outside the dedicated group, see no reason why they should have to limit themselves to the actors already in the company. What happens

> next of course is that those who have committed themselves to the company see the parts they wanted to play and should be playing going to outsiders, new people who have not made and would not make any lengthy commitment. At that point the whole thing begins to break down. I believed that there had to be a core group of directors who helped to create the acting company and committed themselves to it and that the actors must understand from the beginning that they were committed to working with those directors.[136]

Therefore, below the directorate, Nunn established a group of associate directors (the aforementioned Daniels and Davies, plus Barry Kyle, John Caird, Bill Alexander and Adrian Noble) and shared out creative and administrative duties between them. Because Nunn asked his associates to begin as assistant directors, and to make a lasting commitment, he gave the RSC a new cohesion.

Previous page: *The Comedy of Errors* by Shakespeare,
RST, 1976. Francesca Annis (Luciana), Judi Dench (Adriana).
Production: Trevor Nunn. Design: John Napier.
Photograph by Donald Cooper / Alamy.

4 Nunn's Style

As a director Trevor Nunn was versatile and eclectic, a master of both structure and interpretation. The white spaces and clean lines of his production of *The Winter's Tale* in 1969 were carried through into the following year's *Hamlet.* Alan Howard's intelligent, cuttingly ironic Hamlet and Helen Mirren's tender Ophelia were figures in black in a phoney all-white world. The critic Ronald Bryden, who was invited to attend the rehearsals, reported that Nunn saw the play as a study in alienation: 'Hamlet, the thinker, is taught how to feel.' Bryden wrote in his review: 'His madness is not just feigned, it is a Laingian escape from a society built on lunatic deceptions into the lonely sanity of private truth. Between the blacks and whites of public and personal morality, his will is puzzled, until the players burst with a torrent of colour onto the bare Elizabethan platform Christopher Morley has made of the Stratford stage.'[137]

The elegant restraint of this *Hamlet* gave way to the spectacular visuals of *The Romans* in 1972. *Antony and Cleopatra* was later filmed for television, and the popular success of the broadcast gave the Company a boost. Peter Hall, struggling to get the National Theatre up and running on the South Bank, wrote in his *Diaries*: '[Trevor] says people in the RSC offices now say good morning to him in an entirely different way. I wonder if he's right. I think they say good morning in exactly the same way – it's just that he reads it differently.'[138]

Nunn changed direction once more. His Other Place *Macbeth* in 1976 grew out of a frustration with the requirements of the main house. The performance had the directness of a folk tale, with the actors sitting around a bare circle of wooden planks. Its dark, ritualistic atmosphere emanated from the actors' vivid presentation of the text. In its low-key way, it was as important as Brook's *A Midsummer Night's Dream*. The simple but effective device of a single lightbulb hanging above Macbeth's head as he neared his end, would soon be copied by other directors. 'I have never in fact seen the play come across with such throat-grabbing power,' announced Michael Billington in *The Guardian*.[139] Hall, who only gave out praise occasionally in his *Diaries*, admired the production but worried that small-scale Shakespeare was something of a luxury:

> It is magnificent: refreshing, invigorating, utterly clear and original; also the only *Macbeth* I've seen which works. And my admiration for the subtlety of the acting is unbounded. But by doing Shakespeare in a tiny room you do actually sidestep the main problem we moderns have with Shakespeare – rhetoric. We don't like rhetoric, we mistrust it: our actors can't create it, and our audiences don't respond to it. So how on earth do you do a great deal of Shakespeare? It is a problem that will confront us in the Olivier and at the Barbican. The subtlety I saw in this *Macbeth* [...] was only possible because of the scale. In a large theatre something different would have happened – not intellect, but passion; not irony but emotion. [...] For all that, it was an evening that made me proud of my profession again.[140]

Nunn's production of *King Lear*, running concurrently with *Macbeth* but in the main house, was, for Hall, an example of the dilemma of rhetoric: it suggested, he believed, that the principles he had established in the 1960s were slipping: 'There was this slow, over-emphatic, line-breaking delivery of the text. The actors are so busy telling us the ambiguities and the resonances that there is little or no sense of form. You cannot play Shakespeare without a sense of line.'[141] It was inevitable that, over time, verse-speaking would change. For Sally Beauman, the Company's verse-speaking in the 1970s was 'freer, more romantic, and more passionate' than in the 1960s.[142] Nunn, however, still believed in Hall and Barton's rational approach: it had been modified over time, not abandoned, as his *Macbeth* revealed. Ian McKellen, Judi Dench, John Woodvine (Banquo), Bob Peck (Macduff), Roger Rees (Malcolm) and Griffith Jones (Duncan) were outstanding verse-speakers. All of them had learned Hall and Barton's RSC method from Barton himself and from the Company's voice coach Cicely Berry. It is fascinating to learn that Hall was happy with their verse-speaking in the studios but not in the main house. Dench, Peck and Woodvine were in *King Lear*, alongside other actors trained by Hall and Barton in the 1960s – Donald Sinden, Michael Pennington, Michael Williams and Tony Church.

During the 1976 season, Nunn also directed Ian McKellen and Francesca Annis in a vibrant traditional *Romeo and Juliet* and a musical version, highly popular despite the lacklustre songs, of *The Comedy of Errors*. Turning Shakespeare's plays into musicals was one way of trying to solve the problem of rhetoric. If Hall saw the production he didn't comment in his *Diaries*. The musical *Comedy of Errors* was a one-off, no more sustainable than a policy of always performing Shakespeare in the studios.

An intimate *Three Sisters* in the Other Place (1979) was more memorable than a wintry *As You Like It* (1977) and naturalistic *Merry Wives of Windsor* (1979) in the main house. Nunn's concentration on social worlds had given many of his productions a novelistic sweep. In 1980 he went the next step and staged, with John Caird, David Edgar's two-part adaptation of Dickens's *Nicholas Nickleby* (Aldwych). For years he had used wooden, balconied sets and large casts to orchestrate scenes, and *Nickleby* was the climax of this style. It became a phenomenon, touring to New York before being filmed for television.

With *Juno and the Paycock* (1980) and *All's Well That Ends Well* (1981) Nunn took the intimate style of his studio work into the Aldwych and the RST with spellbinding results. *All's Well* was set at the outbreak of the Great War, an elegant Edwardian world of chambermaids and cafés, but also of soldiers disembarking through locomotive steam. The callous snobbery of Mike Gwilym's Bertram made sense in a society of public schoolboy soldiers; Helena's assertion of her rights made sense in the age of the suffragettes. The production also looked to Chekhov, not least in the scenes between Peggy Ashcroft's Countess and Harriet Walter's Helena. After a decade of uncertainty for Nunn, the production was an unexpected vindication of main house Shakespeare.

Hamlet by Shakespeare, RST, 1970. Alan Howard (Hamlet). Production: Trevor Nunn. Design: Christopher Morley. Photograph by Donald Cooper / Alamy.

Hamlet by Shakespeare, RST, 1970. Production: Trevor Nunn. Design: Christopher Morley. Photograph by Donald Cooper / Alamy.

Front: Christopher Gable (Laertes), Peter Egan (Osric), Alan Howard (Hamlet). Behind, left: Terence Taplin (Horatio), David Waller (Claudius). Behind, right: Clement McCallin (Cornelius).

5   Terry Hands and the Main Stage

Trevor Nunn was at the height of his powers as a director of classical texts but he had already made the move into musicals that would end his tenure at the RSC. Andrew Lloyd Webber's *Cats* (1981) started a new phase of his career, and although he remained in joint charge of the RSC until 1986 he was for part of that time away. Terry Hands, joint-artistic director from 1977, took over the primary direction of the Company.

At some point during the 1970s, Terry Hands came to epitomise the idea of the theatre director: enigmatic, European-minded, often dressed in black. His productions of that time, dynamically staged, utilising cavernous darkness and intense white light, showed a mastery of the main stage. Whereas Nunn retreated into the studios, Hands marched with a confident swagger across the biggest stages.

Hands's father was bandmaster of the Duke of Cornwall's Light Infantry. His mother was German. She suffered during the war with her husband and brother fighting on opposite sides (Hands was told that she was Swiss).[143] Hands studied English literature at Birmingham University before training at RADA. While still in his early twenties he founded the Liverpool Everyman (1964) and directed T.S. Eliot's *Murder in the Cathedral*, John Osborne's *Look Back in Anger*, Arnold Wesker's *The Four Seasons*, and *Richard III*. He joined the RSC in 1966 to run the Company's touring group, Theatregoround, and established his reputation with a main stage version of *The Merry Wives of Windsor* (1968) set in period. Hands populated Timothy O'Brien's timbered stage with Bruegel-like figures engaged in the routine activities of everyday life. The production's popularity led to revivals in 1969 and 1975, but Hands was seldom this traditional. Words, images and sound were conjoined into a form of total theatre that, for all its thrilling aggression, represented an articulate response to the themes of the plays. Hands arranged actors and objects on empty stages with a compositional artistry that set him apart from his contemporaries. Farrah created ingenious transformations – floor coverings hoisted to become canopies, or the stage itself rising to form a vertical surface.

Hands directed Helen Mirren in *The Man of Mode* (1971), *The Balcony* (1971) and *Henry VI* (1977); Timothy Dalton and Estelle Kohler in *Romeo and Juliet* (1973); and Alan Howard in *Henry IV*, *Henry V* (1975), *Henry VI*, *Coriolanus* (1977), *Richard II* and *Richard III* (1980). The Hands/Howard history play cycle dominated Stratford in the mid-1970s. With a relatively small number of actors, and sleight of hand, the epic nature of the plays was realised, the action unfolding on a steep rectangular stage that some reviewers compared to the deck of an aircraft carrier; but Hands ensured that the plays' preoccupation with doubt, fear and betrayal undercut the moments of triumph and, in *Henry V*, the rhetorical speeches of the Chorus, which in this context sounded like propaganda. What one would remember most from *Henry V* was the human cost of war, along with the fragile comradery of an army on the march. As dawn broke on the morning of Agincourt, the exhausted soldiers, sleeping against their kit-bags, were called to arms by a cook bashing a ladle against a pot. Hands's unabridged production of the three parts of *Henry VI*, performed in a single day with visceral intensity, was a landmark. Sexually-charged productions of *Twelfth Night* (1979), *As You Like It* (1980) – rarely has this play's rush from winter to spring, from repression to feeling, been so ecstatically realised – and *Troilus and Cressida* (1981) followed.

From 1972 to 78 Hands was a consultant director at the Comédie-Française in Paris,[144] where he directed *Richard III*, *Pericles*, *Twelfth Night*, *Le Cid* and *Murder in the Cathedral*, and married the great actress Ludmila Mikaël[145] (their daughter, Marina Hands, would emerge as a star of French stage and screen in the early 2000s – she joined the Comédie-Française in 2006). On the continent Hands's linguistic skill and production style made him (after Peter Brook) the best placed and most admired British director – he also worked in Vienna at the Burgtheater (*Troilus and Cressida*, *As You Like It*) and in Italy at the Teatro Stabile di Genova (*Women Beware Women*). During one memorable month in Paris in 1976, Hands directed *Twelfth Night* at the Comédie-Française and *Otello* at the Opera, and his RSC *Henry V* visited the Odéon. He worked at the Comédie-Française at a time when Pierre Dux was modernising and revitalising the company. The two became close, and there was a tantalising moment when it looked as if Hands might stay in Paris after Dux's retirement to run the Comédie-Française.[146]

Hands took his experience of working with French actors back to the RSC. His Stratford *Twelfth Night* was a re-working of his Comédie-Française staging of 1976. British productions of *Twelfth Night* are usually centred on the dark comedy of middle-age, the Sir Toby Belch, Aguecheek and Malvolio scenes. In France, where the Englishness of the comedy is difficult to grasp, the misdirected desires of the young female characters dominate. Hands took the opportunity to place Olivia at the centre of the play alongside Viola, making her young, excitable and provocative. As passion spread, Hands's melancholy midwinter setting (snow, bare trees, overturned boxes lit from within to become lanterns) thawed into a tentative spring.

In September 1977, Nunn asked Hands to become co-artistic director of the RSC. Peter Hall, looking for a director capable of staging Shakespeare in the main house, had asked Hands to join him at the National Theatre to run one of two Olivier ensembles (Hall would run the other), and Hands had provisionally accepted. But Hands's passion was for the RSC. Hall felt let down by his Stratford friends, despite the fact that he had tried to capture Hands behind Nunn's back.[147] Nunn and Hands were a formidable duo. By sharing the leadership of the Company they halved the burden.

The talent in the Company was taken for granted back then but amazes today: performing the 1982/83 programme were Jenny Agutter, Alun Armstrong, David Bradley, Ken Bones, John Carlisle, Sinéad Cusack, Jeffery Dench, Michael Gambon, Derek Godfrey, Jonathan Hyde, Derek Jacobi, Sara Kestelman, Alice Krige, Tom Mannion, Helen Mirren, Bob Peck, Pete Postlethwaite, Mark Rylance, Antony Sher, Josette Simon, David Troughton, David Waller and Clive Wood. Hands directed stylish and probing accounts of *Much Ado About Nothing*, *Arden of Faversham* (his first production in the Other Place) and, in London, *Cyrano de Bergerac*, in a new translation by Anthony Burgess. It was a rare French night at the RSC, lyrical and sombre and exquisitely staged and performed. The other plays were entrusted to the Company's young associates. Adrian Noble's main house *King Lear* was presented alongside Edward Bond's *Lear*, staged by Barry Kyle in the studio. Ron Daniels directed Jacobi in *The Tempest* and *Peer Gynt*. Noble followed *King Lear* with an intimate version of *Antony and Cleopatra*, starring Gambon and Mirren, in the studio. The young actress Katy Behean, at the beginning of her RSC career, was a compellingly distinctive presence in a number of roles.

Hands oversaw the difficult move to the Barbican Centre (1982). During the long years of the Barbican's construction, it had become an anachronism. Peter Hall, John Bury and Trevor Nunn had influenced the design of the theatre, but it was placed within a concrete complex that had all the charm of a conference centre. A studio theatre had not been included in the original plans, and the only space suitable was down in the basement: the RSC named it the Pit, and quickly regretted giving up the Warehouse.

Most members of the RSC hated working at the Barbican. People had to make a special effort to get there and were disappointed by the centre's design and facilities. Cut off from the West End, the RSC hoped to attract people who lived or worked in the locality, but without significant success. Hands looked for positives, and hoped that the RSC would, over time, defeat the building only to discover that it was the other way round.

Terry Hands photographed by Reg Wilson in 1969.

6 The Swan

The beginning of Trevor Nunn's break from the RSC coincided with the move to the Barbican and the end of a golden period in the Company's history. Nunn directed *Henry IV*, the Barbican's inaugural production, in his *Nickleby* style. In 1985 he struck a deal with Cameron Mackintosh and staged *Les Misérables* as an RSC production, thereby providing the Company with a valuable source of income. His final act as chief executive was to oversee the opening of the Swan Theatre in 1986. Years earlier he had planned the construction of a new theatre within the shell of the original Shakespeare Memorial Theatre, and the Swan was the result of his vision and perseverance.

The 1926 fire had destroyed the roof and gutted the auditorium but left the shell of the building, including the foyer and gallery rooms, intact. After the construction of the new SMT, the original became a storeroom and eventually the RSC's main rehearsal room, named the Conference Hall. Nunn has admitted that it only dawned on him slowly that the Conference Hall was the original Memorial Theatre, minus its roof, and that the original foyer space was also there once you looked for it.[148] The shape and size of the space, along with its excellent acoustics, led him to the exciting conclusion that the Conference Hall could be reborn as a Jacobean-style galleried playhouse, dedicated to the works of Shakespeare's contemporaries, the persuasive artistic justification for a third Stratford theatre. From the start, Nunn made it clear to his board that he didn't intend for the new theatre to replace the Other Place.

The local architect Michael Reardon delivered an exceptional design (late 1970s), but despite a concerted campaign at home and in America the RSC failed to raise even a fraction of the cost. For years Nunn's dream was placed on hold, waiting for the day when an American multi-billionaire called Frederick Koch would see the model of the Swan in Stratford and say, 'I'd like to pay for that'.[149]

Michael Reardon was inspired by the vertical nature of the space but didn't imitate the theatres of the past. 'I see it as a house where the carpenter has created the world in which the action takes place,' he said.[150] In designing the theatre and its attic rehearsal room, he was influenced by the ducal palaces of northern Italy, particularly those in Sabbioneta and Parma. Trevor Nunn also directed him to look at the theatre of Christ's Hospital in Horsham. Terry Hands would later reveal another influence:

> I remember standing with Trevor and John Barton in John's 15th century dovecote at Hillborough looking up at the walls. Inside it is like a brick colander with each hole a dove's nest. 'That's how it should be,' said someone, 'the walls papered with

people.' The phrase stuck and, thanks to Michael Reardon's loving craft, so did the inspiration.[151]

The combination of the Swan's horseshoe shape, height, bare bricks and wooden galleries provokes a good feeling the moment you enter the auditorium. The four hundred or so spectators line the walls, and surround the platform stage. Those closest sit inches from the stage.

The Swan is an actors' space. With the audience so close and visible, the art of acting takes precedence over directorial concepts. One might think of the studio as a private room, and the Swan as a public forum. Audience members are voyeurs in the Other Place, but participants in the Swan. Many RSC actors found the experience so liberating that they came to dislike working in the main house (an unfortunate consequence of the Swan's success). From the start, directors and designers were less captivated by a theatre that was impossible to disguise or re-configure. Bob Crowley designed the opening show, Shakespeare and Fletcher's *The Two Noble Kinsmen*. He acknowledged the Swan's vertical space by suspending a cage, in which the kinsmen, Hugh Quarshie and Gerard Murphy, were imprisoned, high above the stage and by providing a pole for Imogen Stubbs's Gaoler's Daughter to climb during her mad scene. Unable to transform the acting area into a garden, he used a green ribbon to represent it symbolically. It was beautifully done. However, Crowley was quite blunt about the limitations: 'The problem I have with it as a designer is that it imposes itself, hugely, and no matter what you do, you design against it, at your peril':

> Theatres, and specifically the Swan, have sometimes been described as creating 'sacred spaces'. I think if one wants to create a sacred space that's up to directors, designers and actors together to create that feeling. If an architect has created that feeling to begin with, it just limits your scope and the possibilities of doing other forms of theatre. And somehow when I think of the Swan, the theatre is what I remember most.[152]

Visual spectacle was never part of the Swan's brief. Nunn said of the new theatre:

> It should contain the adrenalin you get when a relatively large number of people are in direct contact both with the actor and with one another. It will be a theatre where the dramatic effects are achieved by the actor, who should be able to engage the whole audience with the flicker of an eyebrow. It can never be a theatre of illusion. [...] We are not budgeting for visual extravagance. The audience will be so close to the action that I do not believe they will miss the 'design concept' they might expect in a proscenium theatre.[153]

The Swan and its rehearsal room cost a modest two million pounds to build. It opened, under the direction of Barry Kyle, in 1986. The joint RST/Swan building wasn't really big enough to contain two theatres presenting shows at the same time. Imogen Stubbs described the backstage 'bustle and mess': 'When you exit you have to go through two doors and up some steps. And on the other side of the doors, you've got the other play happening in the main house. It's very hard to concentrate on your character. Just a stream of people going to the café on the one side, and the dominating acting force of the main house on the other side.'[154] The largely unknown *Two Noble Kinsmen*, a play with two prominent young female roles, the Gaoler's Daughter and Emilia (played by Amanda Harris), seemed as revelatory as the theatre in which it was being performed. You could sense the tension in the actors, the nervousness, as they took to the stage, the energy that passed between them and the watching crowd. It was, as Nunn and Hands predicted, a different experience from the studio: more conspiratorial, more intimate.

True to Nunn's brief for the new theatre, the first years saw performances of important neglected plays. The major works of Marlowe and Jonson were staged, alongside masterpieces by John Ford and John Webster. If the Swan gave the RSC a new dimension in terms of repertoire, it also inspired some of the Company's most revealing productions of Shakespeare, Chekhov and Ibsen – Deborah Warner's *Titus Andronicus* (1987), Sam Mendes's *Troilus and Cressida* (1990), Terry Hands's *The Seagull* (1990), Adrian Noble's

The Cherry Orchard (1995), John Barton's *Peer Gynt* (1994) and Noble's *Little Eyolf* (1996).

'The Swan,' Terry Hands wrote, 'is truly a place for people not things, and the audience is its architecture. The actors can do anything except for one minute forget that they are actors performing to and for an audience. It is this realism, this honesty, which makes the Swan such a thrilling theatre.' For this reason, Nunn and Hands were delighted with the Swan as a space for Shakespeare's comedies and romances. They were less sure about performing tragedy there. Bob Crowley's thoughts on the Swan have remained valid, for although there have been great productions (see above), they have been few and far between, particularly during the last ten years. The issue became more worrying when the main house was rebuilt as a second Swan, meaning that Stratford had no arena for visual theatre. This was not the choice of Nunn or Hands.

7 The End of the Nunn/Hands Era

The 1986 season was Trevor Nunn's last as joint-artistic director. It was a strong year. Sinéad Cusack played opposite Jeremy Irons in *The Rover* and Jonathan Pryce in *Macbeth*. Sean Bean and Niamh Cusack were a lyrical but understated *Romeo and Juliet* in modern-dress in a Verona of sports cars and scooters, and Michael Kitchen, making his Stratford debut, was sardonic, droll and Pinteresque as Mercutio, Bolingbroke and a cockney Hogarth in Nick Dear's *The Art of Success*. There was an abundance of talent at the core of the company: Pete Postlethwaite, Gerard Murphy, Hugh Quarshie, Henry Goodman, David Haig, David Troughton, Roger Demeger, Joe Melia and Nicholas Woodeson were in danger of tripping over each other. As well as Imogen Stubbs and Amanda Harris, emerging players included Janet McTeer, Simon Russell Beale, Imelda Staunton, Penny Downie, Nathaniel Parker and Joely Richardson. In a prominent example of how the RSC's need for sponsorship sometimes clashed with the principles of its leading actors, Pryce threatened to withdraw if the Company didn't end its association with Barclays Bank, sponsor of *Macbeth*.

Nunn directed an exuberant production of Thomas Heywood's *The Fair Maid of the West* in the Swan and then effectively stepped down. Many of the major actors of the Nunn years – Helen Mirren, Ben Kingsley, Patrick Stewart, David Suchet, Bob Peck, Judi Dench, Roger Rees, Mike Gwilym – also departed. Terry Hands continued as artistic director, supported by Adrian Noble (who was given oversight of the 1988 Stratford season), Ron Daniels, Barry Kyle, John Caird, Bill Alexander and the Company's long-serving general manager David Brierley. The RSC grew in size during the 1980s. The opening of the Swan and its London equivalent, the Mermaid, in 1987, meant that Hands was running six theatres at a time when the RSC's grant was frozen. A government inquiry into the RSC had concluded, in 1983, that the Company was well-managed and under-funded and recommended that its subsidy should be increased and index-linked,[155] but ministers and officials were soon ignoring this inconvenient truth.

The RSC withdrew from the Mermaid in 1988 (expansion only made economic sense in the short term), and was forced to close the Other Place a year later when Stratford council, after years of concern over health and safety, finally refused to renew the performance licence. In 1989, the much-loved shed, so significant in the history of British theatre since the war, was dismantled and sold off to a farmer. The RSC decided to sell most of the site (known as the Paddock) to a housing developer and use the money to build a new theatre on the section of land it retained.[156] The decision was pragmatic but surely wrong. If there really was no way around the health and safety issues, the RSC should have used the shed for another purpose and built a modern replica on the same site. 'You could *feel* the trees and riverside pleasures outside,' wrote Michael Coveney of the tin shed.[157] Its redbrick replacement, designed by Michael Reardon, would be almost as basic but entirely devoid of atmosphere or pleasure.

The final production at the Other Place was meant to be the premiere of Timberlake Wertenbaker's *The Love of the Nightingale*. It followed a fine production of *King John* by Deborah Warner and closed the 1988-89 season with a melancholy sigh. It was a Greek tale of rape and revenge given a feminist reading and in such a small space it achieved a sickly intimacy. Reviews were mixed despite a powerful central performance by Katy Behean. The indisposition of Peter Lennon meant that Nicholas Woodeson stepped in during the run to read the part of Tereus. Garry Hynes's staging was a little too elegant, the actors costumed in stylish blue: in London, in the Pit, it was re-thought and delivered with a savagery that revealed a finer work. The closure of TOP inevitably over-shadowed the play. Michael Coveney wrote in his review for *The Financial Times*:

> We trooped out after 90 minutes into a dank and balmy Stratford night of soggy leaves and eerie riverside echoes as the transformed rape victim sang to her dead nephew accompanied by a flute. All very sad, very downbeat. It has become increasingly difficult for the RSC to wheedle a performing licence out of the local authorities for a venue that palpably does not conform to the highest safety standards. But which valuable little theatre ever did? The closure is a tragedy, and plans to re-open another Other Place in the immediate environment in 1990 do not guarantee the indefinable magic that has informed the McKellen/Dench *Macbeth*, Alan Howard in *The Forest*, Cheryl Campbell in *A Doll's House*, *Les Liaisons dangereuses* and, this season, *King John*. As the RSC's new plays policy dwindles in confusion, Miss Wertenbaker's piece, I'm afraid, only goes to prove another fact of TOP lore: good writers have rarely done their best work in it. The place has been a forcing house of classical reappraisals and a dynamically intimate acting style that has threatened to overwhelm the rhetorical requirements and challenges of the main stage.[158]

Soon after the end of the season, Terry Hands decided that TOP deserved a much bigger send-off that would close the circle. He asked Nunn to direct Ian McKellen as Iago in *Othello*. A short run of performances was squeezed in during the summer before the theatre was demolished. McKellen was joined by Willard White, Imogen Stubbs and Zoë Wanamaker. The setting seemed to be a military outpost in the deep South during the aftermath of the American Civil War, a place parched by heat. Nunn used the claustrophobic, nowhere to escape, Other Place to maximum effect, increasing the tension by slow degrees for over four hours until it was almost unbearable. The great scene between Desdemona and Emilia had never been more intimately or poignantly played than here. Stubbs turned the willow song into a plaintive blues that she was too fearful to end and Wanamaker was exhausted by sadness: as spoken by Wanamaker, the speech 'What is it that they do when they change us for others?' became the play's heart and soul. Michael Coveney wrote of McKellen's pallid sociopath: 'His suburban rapacity for promotion is almost a comic symptom, a vaudevillian impression enhanced by his Führer-style moustache and railway porter's cap.'[159]

By 1990 the RSC's financial situation was so grave that Hands closed the Barbican and Pit theatres from November to March 1991. This was a direct challenge to the Arts Council and the government, a risky policy of brinkmanship that succeeded because the government couldn't allow a flagship arts organisation to go under. The RSC's grant was increased and the Barbican Theatre re-opened in the spring. Hands took the brunt of media criticism. *The Sunday Times*, in particular, had been openly hostile to Nunn and Hands for some years. There was something intriguingly personal about its journalists' sustained campaign against the directors: the tone undermined any sound points they were making.[160] The press was right to express legitimate concerns over the quality of verse-speaking and the RSC's decision to stage musicals; but too little attention was given to the fact that the RSC was underfunded. The Company's subsidy remained way below that awarded to the National, and the staging of money-making musicals should have been viewed in that context. Quite often, the writers of articles on the RSC would bemoan the poor standard of the Company's work without seeming to know what was actually happening on the stage. For instance, attacks intensified during 1989, when Hands presented in London four undoubtedly great productions in a row – Trevor Nunn's *Othello*, Adrian Noble's *The Plantagenets* and *The Master Builder*, and Ron Daniels's *Hamlet* with Mark Rylance. Success, of course, is temporary. Howard Brenton's *Moscow Gold*, Anthony Burgess's *A Clockwork Orange* and David Edgar's *The Strange Case of Dr Jekyll and Mr Hyde*, all presented at the Barbican in 1990/91, were honourable failures.

When, in April 1989, Hands announced that he would step

down as artistic director at the end of the 1990 season it was his own choice. The fact that the chairman, Sir Geoffrey Cass,[161] didn't attempt to persuade Hands to stay may suggest, though, that the board was ambivalent. Hands and Cass agreed that twelve years was a long time to run a theatre, and believed they had identified the right candidate to take over – Adrian Noble. Should Cass have persuaded Hands to continue? Probably. His last years in charge were exceptional: he brought in important new talent (Nicholas Hytner, Deborah Warner, Sam Mendes, Danny Boyle), brought to the fore a new generation of actors (including Ralph Fiennes, Amanda Root, Simon Russell Beale, Amanda Harris, Linus Roache, Imogen Stubbs, Mark Rylance, Richard McCabe), and premiered Peter Flannery's *Singer* in the Swan. *Singer* was a rare beast, a new play that was large in scale and distinctive in character.

The song that ended the 1990 *Love's Labour's Lost*, Hands's farewell to the RST, came to a surprising climax when Richard Ridings's slow-witted Dull produced a pitch-perfect falsetto note. The 1990 ensemble was one of the most talented since the 1970s. Fiennes, Simon Russell Beale and Amanda Root starred in *Love's Labour's Lost*, John Wood played *King Lear* for Nicholas Hytner, and Alex Jennings and Linus Roache were outstanding in Ron Daniels's expressionistic *Richard II*. As good as these productions were, it was the work in the Swan that capped the season, not least because it was here that the extraordinary young trio of Fiennes, Beale and Roache really made their mark. Perhaps one would need to go back to 1963, the year of Ian Holm, David Warner and Ian Richardson, to find an equivalent moment. Linus Roache was the chillingly enigmatic centre of Nick Dear's version of Tirso de Molina's *The Last Days of Don Juan*, directed with visual flair by Danny Boyle; Ralph Fiennes was lyrical and grave in *Troilus and Cressida*, directed by Sam Mendes; and Simon Russell Beale was vividly scabrous as Thersites in *Troilus* and poignantly crushed as Konstantin in *The Seagull*, directed by Hands. *Troilus and Cressida*, which also starred Amanda Root, Norman Rodway, Ciarán Hinds and David Troughton, had a lucidity of expression that equalled Hands's *The Seagull*. The latter's cast included Roger Allam, Susan Fleetwood, Amanda Root and Katy Behean.

Despite the success of the 1990 season, it was widely felt that the

RSC faced an uncertain future. Following the announcement of his departure, Terry Hands published an article in *The Guardian* in which, rightly worried about the future, he affirmed the values of the RSC. It was as if he was sending a message to his successors when he wrote:

> The RSC has never had stars, nor has it ever been without them. Simply they are more often of today and tomorrow than yesterday. [...] Above all I shall miss the sense of family. [...] That is what is unique about the RSC and that is what is most unpopular in these fast-food, tomorrow's-chip-paper times. It is a real company with as much concern for the nursery slopes as the giant slaloms. It must be preserved. It is irreplaceable.[162]

Previous page: *Troilus and Cressida* by Shakespeare, Swan, 1990. Simon Russell Beale (Thersites). Production: Sam Mendes. Design: Anthony Ward. Photograph: Trinity Mirror / Alamy.

Above: *The Last Days of Don Juan* by Nick Dear, Swan, 1990. Production: Danny Boyle. Design: Kandis Cook. Centre: Catherine White (Aminta), Linus Roache (Don Juan), Lloyd Hutchinson (Ripio). Photograph by Donald Cooper / Alamy.

8 Nunn/Hands's RSC: Some Representative Actors

When Trevor Nunn took charge of the RSC, the Company contained, at its core, a group of talented and committed actors of his own generation who were ready to step into the spotlight.

The young Judi Dench played Anya in Michel Saint-Denis's *The Cherry Orchard*, Isabella in *Measure for Measure*, Titania, and Dorcas Bellboys in *A Penny for a Song* at the RSC in 1961/62. She was petite and seemingly malleable, and for some years would be overshadowed by her contemporaries Vanessa Redgrave, Maggie Smith and Glenda Jackson. But in 1968 Judi Dench shattered her image as Sally Bowles in *Cabaret* (Palace Theatre). It was the first indication of the range of emotion at her disposal, and of her boldness (she was not a natural singer). Trevor Nunn brought her back into the RSC and asked her to play both Hermione and Perdita in his production of *The Winter's Tale*, Bianca in Terry Hands's *Women Beware Women* and Viola in John Barton's *Twelfth Night*. She won acclaim for the quality she brought to Shakespeare's heroines, a blend of tenderness and vivacity all her own. The expressiveness of her voice and her ability to time lines and looks were at the heart of her appeal. The next ten years witnessed remarkable combinations across seasons: in 1971, Portia in *The Merchant of Venice* and the Duchess in *The Duchess of Malfi*; in 1976/77, Beatrice in *Much Ado About Nothing*, Lady Macbeth, Adriana in *The Comedy of Errors*, Regan in *King Lear* and Lona Hessel in Ibsen's *Pillars of the Community*; and, in 1979/80, Imogen in *Cymbeline* and Juno in *Juno and the Paycock*. Judi Dench was deeply affecting as Beatrice, opposite Donald Sinden, sublimely funny as the exasperated Adriana, and shockingly severe as Lady Macbeth, encapsulating the character's decline in a single silent scream. In 1984/85, at the Barbican, she played the title role in *Mother Courage* and Amy in Harley Granville-Barker's *Waste*.

Judi Dench married Michael Williams, her RSC contemporary, in 1971. Michael Williams was a performer who, the moment he walked onto a stage, made a connection with spectators based on either melancholy or joy. His Shakespearean work combined feeling, wit and personality. In his first years with the Company, from 1963, he played Puck and Rosencrantz for Peter Hall, Oswald in *King Lear* for Peter Brook, and Dromio in *The Comedy of Errors* for Clifford Williams. He was next Petruchio to Janet Suzman's Kate and Troilus to Helen Mirren's Cressida. He was both Eric Porter's and Donald Sinden's Fool (in 1968 and 76 respectively). He was a member of Peter Brook's experimental group, appearing in *Marat/Sade* and *US* (it was Williams who set fire to the 'butterfly'). In 1976, as well as playing the Fool in *King Lear*, he repeated his masterly Dromio.

Alan Howard joined the RSC in 1966, having appeared at the Royal Court in Arnold Wesker's trilogy *Roots* and at Chichester under Laurence Olivier. Although young, he was already a wise classical actor, at ease with complex language and able to project in the old fashioned sense. For Nunn, between 1966 and 70, Howard played Lussurioso in *The Revenger's Tragedy*, Edgar in *King Lear*, Benedick to Janet Suzman's Beatrice, and Hamlet. He was Oberon in Peter Brook's *A Midsummer Night's Dream*. This iconic production was not only about Brook's concept; it was also about the sound of Howard's voice. The history plays dominated the rest of his long RSC career. Between 1975 and 81, in productions by Terry Hands, he played Shakespeare's English kings in an epic style that was also sardonic, ambiguous and questioning.

Patrick Stewart and Ben Kingsley joined the RSC the same year as Howard, and performed alongside him in *The Revenger's Tragedy* and *A Midsummer Night's Dream*. Stewart's extraordinary range of roles included Witness 3 in Peter Brook's production of Peter Weiss's *The Investigation*, the First Player in the David Warner *Hamlet*, the title role in *King John*, Stephano in *The Tempest*, Cassius, Astrov in *Uncle Vanya*, Shakespeare in Edward Bond's *Bingo*, and Shylock. Kingsley matched Stewart. Following his performance as Demetrius in the *Dream*, he played Ariel in *The Tempest* and Sintsov in Gorky's *Enemies*. He became involved in the Company's small-scale work and starred as Hamlet in Buzz Goodbody's 1975 production. Kingsley continued at the RSC – Ford in *The Merry Wives of Windsor*, Brecht's Baal, Brutus, Squeers in *Nicholas*

Nickleby – until the role of Gandhi in Richard Attenborough's film transformed his career.

Helen Mirren was also in *The Revenger's Tragedy*, in 1967, during her first Stratford season. She was very young and glamorous. A tabloid newspaper, responding to her nude scenes in Michael Powell's *Age of Consent* (1969) and Ken Russell's *Savage Messiah* (1971), quickly labelled her 'Sex Queen of the RSC'. But Mirren shied away from this kind of attention. For more than a decade she concentrated on classical roles at the RSC: Cressida, Hero in *Much Ado About Nothing*, Susie Monican in Sean O'Casey's *The Silver Tassie*, Ophelia to Howard's Hamlet, Lady Anne in *Richard III*, Julia in *The Two Gentlemen of Verona*, Tatyana in Gorky's *Enemies*, Harriet in Etherege's *The Man of Mode*, Strindberg's Miss Julie, Lady Macbeth opposite Nicol Williamson, and Queen Margaret in the three parts of *Henry VI*. When she wasn't performing with the RSC she was travelling across north Africa with Peter Brook's international troupe. She returned in 1982/83 to play a mercurial Cleopatra opposite Michael Gambon in Adrian Noble's production of *Antony and Cleopatra*, and Moll Cutpurse in Middleton and Dekker's *The Roaring Girl*.

Like Helen Mirren, Roger Rees started his RSC career in 1967 and was in *The Revenger's Tragedy* (in an unnamed role). He progressed to supporting roles, but it wasn't until 1976 that his expressively energetic style (he possessed the ability to shift mood line by line) was given full reign in both comedic and dramatic roles: Benvolio in *Romeo and Juliet*, Malcolm in the Other Place *Macbeth*, the Young Shepherd in *The Winter's Tale*, and, especially, Antipholus of Syracuse in Nunn's *Comedy of Errors*. He went on to play Tusenbach in *Three Sisters* and Aguecheek in *Twelfth Night* for the first small-scale tour, Posthumus to Judi Dench's Imogen in *Cymbeline*, Podsekalnikov in Nikolai Erdman's *The Suicide*, and the title role in *Nicholas Nickleby*. He returned in 1984 to play Hamlet and Berowne in *Love's Labour's Lost*.

Mike Gwilym played Roger Rees's twin in *The Comedy of Errors*. He brought to his classical characters – Edgar in Buzz Goodbody's *King Lear*, Vlass in *Summerfolk*, Costard in *Love's Labour's Lost*, Troilus, Surly in *The Alchemist*, and Achilles/Orestes in John Barton's trilogy *The Greeks* – a tense physicality, making them seem perpetually on the edge of an outburst. During his last phase of work with the Company, 1981/82, he was angst-ridden and malevolent as Benjamin Wouldbe in Farquhar's *The Twin Rivals*, sinister as Oberon, heartless as Bertram in *All's Well That Ends Well* and hilariously paranoid as a scene-stealing Pistol in *Henry IV*.

Emrys James was a member of the RSC from 1968, working frequently for Terry Hands. Welsh working-class toughness and Welsh lyricism were apparent in many of his performances. His prickly personality gave an edge to his acting, and he could be intimidating. Among his achievements were a melancholy Feste in John Barton's *Twelfth Night* and a chilling Iago in *Othello*. He was a commanding figure in Hands's productions of the histories, playing the title role in *Henry IV* and York in *Henry VI*. Brenda Bruce played Mistress Quickly in the histories. She was the ideal vessel for Shakespeare's humanism, the RSC's resident Mistress Page in *The Merry Wives of Windsor* (performing the role for John Blatchley in 1964 and for Terry Hands in 1968 and 1975), Dionyza in *Pericles*, Paulina in *The Winter's Tale*, Maria in *Twelfth Night*, Queen Elizabeth in *Richard III*, Gertrude in *Hamlet*, Queen Margaret in *Richard III*, and the Nurse in *Romeo and Juliet*.

Michael Pennington first appeared at the RSC in 1965/66, playing Dumaine in *Love's Labour's Lost*, Fortinbras in the David Warner *Hamlet* and Stark in Peter Weiss's *The Investigation*. A leading player of the years 1974 to 1981, he was Angelo in *Measure for Measure*, Johnnie in David Rudkin's *Afore Night Come*, Mercutio in *Romeo and Juliet*, Hector in *Troilus and Cressida*, Major Rolfe in David Edgar's *Destiny*, Edgar in the Donald Sinden *King Lear*, Berowne in *Love's Labour's Lost*, and Hamlet – the immaculate verse-speaking and gimmick-free characterisation made the interpretation seem old-fashioned when it was anything but. If a scholarly, carefully considered approach to the craft of acting defined Pennington's elegant style, he was never dryly cerebral.

Susan Fleetwood made a bold impression during her first two seasons, 1968 and 69, playing a very young Regan in Trevor Nunn's *King Lear*, both Marina and Thaisa in Terry Hands's *Pericles*, and Isabella in *Women Beware Women*. Among her subsequent roles were Portia, the Chorus Leader in *Murder in the Cathedral*, the Princess of France in *Love's Labour's Lost*, Kate to Alan Bates's

Petruchio in *The Taming of the Shrew*, Imogen in *Cymbeline*, and Rosalind in Hands's *As You Like It*.

John Wood was one of the RSC's most distinctive players of the 1970s, a tall, lean, edgy ironist whose relish for words found a perfect outlet in a disparate choice of roles: Bardin in Gorky's *Enemies*, Sir Fopling Flutter in Terry Hands's production of *The Man of Mode*, Richard Rowan in James Joyce's *Exiles*, Brutus in Trevor Nunn's production of *Julius Caesar*, the title role in *Sherlock Holmes*, Henry Carr, a part written for him, in Stoppard's *Travesties*, and the title role in Chekhov's *Ivanov*. He returned a decade later to play Prospero and Lear for Nicholas Hytner, Solness in *The Master Builder* for Adrian Noble, and Don Armado in *Love's Labour's Lost* for Terry Hands.

Like Patrick Stewart, David Suchet, who joined the Company in 1973, was a charismatic leading actor who played many supporting and character roles along the way. His work included Tybalt in *Romeo and Juliet*, the Fool in *King Lear*, Caliban in *The Tempest*, Grumio in *The Taming of the Shrew*, Sir Nathaniel in *Love's Labour's Lost*, Pompey in Peter Brook's *Antony and Cleopatra*, Bolingbroke in *Richard II*, Shylock, Achilles in *Troilus and Cressida*, and Iago to Ben Kingsley's Othello.

Ian McKellen was never a fully committed RSC member, but he dominated the Company's 1976/77 season, playing Romeo and Leontes in the main house and Macbeth at the Other Place, directed by Trevor Nunn. McKellen, in general a master technician specialising in intellectually gripping concepts, seemed dangerously possessed as Macbeth. The following year, in London, he added Face in *The Alchemist*, Alex in Tom Stoppard and André Previn's *Every Good Boy Deserves Favour*, Bernick in Ibsen's *Pillars of the Community*, and Langevin in Brecht's *The Days of the Commune*. For the RSC's first small-scale tour, which he led, he played Sir Toby Belch in *Twelfth Night* and Andrei in *Three Sisters*. He returned in 1989 to star in the final production at the Other Place, *Othello*. McKellen's Iago – a womanish NCO whose psychotic nature was convincingly hidden from the other characters while, paradoxically, being apparent in the most ordinary of gestures (for instance, the obsessive way he tidied the bunks in the barracks) – was among his most original creations.

McKellen's Juliet was Francesca Annis. Her time with the RSC was regrettably short, given the quality of her performances between 1974 and 77: as well as Juliet, she played Isabella in *Measure for Measure*, Cressida, and Luciana in Nunn's musical version of *The Comedy of Errors*.

Anton Lesser had only recently left drama school when Terry Hands selected him to play the pivotal role of Richard of Gloucester in the three parts of *Henry VI* (1977). His boyish Richard was an electrifying creation. He went on to play Romeo, Troilus, Richard III, Bolingbroke, Petruchio, and Richard again (in *The Plantagenets*). Alongside the Shakespeares, Lesser starred in David Rudkin's *The Sons of Light*, Strindberg's *The Dance of Death*, and Edward Bond's *The Fool*.

Sinéad Cusack first appeared at the RSC in 1975, as Grace in *London Assurance*, but it was during the years 1979 to 86 that she came into her own as one of the Company's leading actresses: Isabella in *Measure for Measure*, Celia in *As You Like It*, Elizaveta in Gorky's *The Children of the Sun*, Lady Anne to Alan Howard's Richard III, Evadne in *The Maid's Tragedy*, Portia, Beatrice to Derek Jacobi's Benedick, Kate in *The Taming of the Shrew*, and Lady Macbeth to Jonathan Pryce's Macbeth.

Pryce and Cusack made a volatile couple. Unpredictability had always been Pryce's calling card. At the beginning of the RSC's 1978 production of *The Taming of the Shrew* an unruly drunk invaded the auditorium and wrecked the set – he turned out to be Pryce's Petruchio. Pryce spoke Shakespeare's lines in a jagged mannered style. His Petruchio was a bully without redeeming features. That season, he also played Angelo in *Measure for Measure* and Octavius in Peter Brook's *Antony and Cleopatra*.

Juliet Stevenson joined the RSC the same year as Pryce. She played Curtis in *The Taming of the Shrew* and Iras in *Antony and Cleopatra*. Her talent was quickly recognised. She was striking as a young Isabella in Adrian Noble's *Measure for Measure*, and as Titania in *A Midsummer Night's Dream*, Susan in *The Witch of Edmonton*, the loyal maid in Stephen Poliakoff's *Breaking the Silence*, and the destroyed Madame de Tourvel in Christopher Hampton's *Les Liaisons dangereuses*.

Juliet Stevenson possessed the charisma and distinctiveness to make Shakespeare's heroines unfamiliar, as did Harriet Walter. Harriet Walter came to notice as Jonathan Pryce's Ophelia at the Royal Court. A member of the RSC from 1980, she played Madeleine Bray in *Nicholas Nickleby*, Helena in Trevor Nunn's *All's Well That Ends Well*, Lady Percy in *Henry IV*, Skinner in Howard Barker's *The Castle*, Viola, Imogen in *Cymbeline*, the Duchess of Malfi, Lady Macbeth, Beatrice, and Cleopatra.

Harriet Walter's Macbeth was Antony Sher. A talented artist and writer, Sher constructed characters from images, changing his appearance for each role and deliberately submerging his own personality. This approach looked back to Laurence Olivier, but Sher came up with revisionist interpretations. At the RSC he was drawn to outsiders and anti-heroes, beginning with the Fool in Adrian Noble's production of *King Lear*. The physical appearance of his Richard III grew from the image of a 'bottled spider' (hence the crutches) and a study of real deformities. It was a performance of relentless energy and the blackest humour. Sher went on to play an intense, unassimilated Shylock, deliberately unsympathetic, in *The Merchant of Venice*, Vindice in *The Revenger's Tragedy*, the title role in Peter Flannery's *Singer*, Marlowe's Tamburlaine the Great, Leontes in *The Winter's Tale*, and Iago.

Kenneth Branagh starred in Adrian Noble's dark, anti-war staging of *Henry V* in 1984. The twenty-four-year-old was suddenly the 'new Olivier'. He could command a big stage, but other similarities were merely superficial. For a few years he ran his own touring company, Renaissance. In 1992 he returned to the RSC to play Hamlet. It was his best work.

Gerard Murphy first appeared with the RSC in 1973, playing minor roles in Trevor Nunn's *The Romans* and David Rudkin's *Cries from Casement*. Having made his name at the Glasgow Citizens' as a visceral performer of some originality, he re-joined the RSC in 1980: Johnny Boyle in *Juno and the Paycock*, the Young Shepherd in *The Winter's Tale*, Frank opposite Harriet Walter and Juliet Stevenson in *The Witch of Edmonton*, and Hal in Nunn's production of the two parts of *Henry IV*. Murphy, fair-haired and thickset, held his own against the svelte Timothy Dalton and later Hugh Quarshie (playing Hotspur). His strikingly original Hal was a rough and bitter creation. Among Murphy's later RSC roles were

Oberon, and Solange in the Genet double-bill of *Deathwatch* and *The Maids*, which he also co-directed. He brought a Presbyterian preacher's intensity to the title role in *Doctor Faustus*, played Petruchio without any notion of political correctness, and as Oedipus in *The Thebans*, a hunched, mud-caked figure led by Joanne Pearce's Antigone, presented an unforgettable image of misery and stoicism.

Gerard Murphy and Hugh Quarshie were reunited for *The Two Noble Kinsmen*, the Swan's opening production. Quarshie was an arrogant, image-conscious Tybalt in *Romeo and Juliet*, and brought considerable presence and depth to Banquo in the Jonathan Pryce *Macbeth*, Belville in *The Rover*, and Mark Antony in Peter Hall's *Julius Caesar*. In 1995/96 he was a cool, stylish Mephistopheles in Michael Bogdanov's modern-dress production of *Faust*.

Imogen Stubbs gave an unforgettable performance in *The Two Noble Kinsmen*, her first appearance with the Company. There was a subtle amalgam of humour and longing in her interpretation of the Gaoler's Daughter, a lovesick girl descending into madness. She played the mad scene as though transported by the fantasy (the Gaoler's Daughter believes herself to be in the crow's nest of a ship) and the pity, tapping into real grief. She spoke the lines with a skill of spontaneity and emphasis, so that decades later they still belonged to her voice ('they shall stand in fire up to the navel and in ice up to th' heart, and there th'offending part burns, and the deceiving part freezes...'). She was next Helena in *The Rover* and Queen Isabel in *Richard II*, playing opposite Jeremy Irons, and a fine Desdemona in Trevor Nunn's *Othello*: in the intimate Other Place, where you could smell her perfume and the lemonade in her glass, her performance was beautifully modulated and touching.

The young Ralph Fiennes performed a grave and edgy Henry VI in *The Plantagenets*, and went on to star as Troilus, Edmund in *King Lear* and Berowne in *Love's Labour's Lost*. Few of Fiennes's contemporaries spoke Shakespeare's verse with such assurance. His performances, although effortlessly stylish, had an undertone of gravitas.

Among the other actors who stood out during the Nunn and Hands years (some having started under Peter Hall; others continuing under Adrian Noble) were Norman Rodway (Thersites in

Troilus and Cressida, Richard III, Captain Boyle in *Juno and the Paycock*), Sara Kestelman (Titania, Lady Macbeth, Goneril in *King Lear*), Mary Rutherford (Hermia in *A Midsummer Night's Dream*), Gemma Jones (Titania, Hermione in *The Winter's Tale*, Katherine in *Henry VIII*), Colin Blakely (Deeley in Pinter's *Old Times*, Titus Andronicus), Richard Pasco (Becket in *Murder in the Cathedral*, Richard II, Bolingbroke, Timon of Athens), Alun Armstrong (Squeers in *Nicholas Nickleby*, Petruchio, Leontes, Thersites), John Carlisle (Ulysses in *Troilus and Cressida*, Oberon, Iachimo in *Cymbeline*), Richard Griffiths (Bottom, Volpone, Henry VIII), Bob Peck (Iago, Macbeth, Caliban), John Woodvine (Falstaff, Malvolio), Zoë Wanamaker (Viola, Emilia in *Othello*), Cherie Lunghi (Cordelia, Viola), Alan Rickman (Jaques, Achilles, Valmont in *Les liaisons dangereuses*), David Threlfall (Mark Antony in *Julius Caesar*, Spike in *Nicholas Nickleby*), Lesley Manville (Phebe in *As You Like It*, Cécile in *Les liaisons dangereuses*); Geoffrey Freshwater (a myriad of character roles over a period of thirty-five years, including Elbow in *Measure for Measure*, Borachio in *Much Ado About Nothing*, Lenin in Stoppard's *Travesties*, Philip of France in *King John*), David Killick (Ross in *Macbeth*, Don Diego in Tirso de Molina's *The Last Days of Don Juan*, Boyet in *Love's Labour's Lost*, Aslak in *Peer Gynt*), Graham Turner (Rowland in *The Witch of Edmonton*, Davy in *Henry IV*, Peter Simple in *The Merry Wives of Windsor*, the Young Shepherd in *The Winter's Tale*), Michael Gambon (King Lear, Antony), Malcolm Storry (Kent in *King Lear*, Aufidius in *Coriolanus*, Manik in *Singer*), Katy Behean (Solveig in *Peer Gynt*, Belinda in *The Man of Mode*, Masha in *The Seagull*), Roger Allam (Mercutio, Brutus), Pete Postlethwaite (Bottom), Tom Wilkinson (Horatio, Antonio in *The Merchant of Venice*), Mark Rylance (Ariel, Hamlet, Romeo), Cécile Paoli (Katharine in the Kenneth Branagh *Henry V*, Mila in *The Desert Air*, Kara in *The Party*), Penny Downie (Lady Anne in *Richard III*, Sarah in *The Art of Success*, Queen Margaret in *The Plantagenets*), Niamh Cusack (Desdemona, Juliet, Jane in *The Art of Success*, Rosalind), Sean Bean (Romeo, Spencer in *The Fair Maid of the West*), Michael Kitchen (Mercutio, Bolingbroke, Hogarth in *The Art of Success*), Amanda Root (Juliet, Cressida, Rosaline in *Love's Labour's Lost*), and Linus Roache (Mark Antony in *Julius Caesar*, Don Juan, Edgar in *King Lear*).

The RSC benefited greatly from the commitment of its senior character actors. The long, distinguished career of Sebastian Shaw spanned seventy years. Shaw made his debut at Stratford at the age of twenty in 1926 and was still walking its stage in his eighties, a grandly charismatic elder statesman. During the period 1966 to 76, he played Duncan to Paul Scofield's Macbeth, Friar Laurence, Gloucester to Eric Porter's Lear, Ulysses in *Troilus and Cressida*, Vincentio to Estelle Kohler's Isabella in *Measure for Measure*, Polonius to Alan Howard's Hamlet, General Pechenegov in Gorky's *Enemies*, and Cymbeline. During the 1980s, he was Charles VI in Adrian Noble's *Henry V*, and the First Gravedigger in *Hamlet*.

David Waller joined the RSC in 1962 and remained a member for twenty-four of the next twenty-nine years. It is impossible to consider the RSC of this period without reference to him. He was Bottom in Peter Brook's *A Midsummer Night's Dream*, Duff opposite Peggy Ashcroft in Harold Pinter's *Landscape*, Pandarus to the Cressidas of Helen Mirren and Francesca Annis, Kent and Gloucester to the Lears of Eric Porter and Michael Gambon, and Claudius to the Hamlet of Alan Howard. He was in *The Wars of the Roses* (1964) and *The Plantagenets* (1988). For such a commanding actor, Waller was a natural clown. If that famous Bottom is the best example, he was also the First Gravedigger in the David Warner *Hamlet*, Dull in *Love's Labour's Lost*, and Dogberry in *Much Ado About Nothing*.

Jeffery Dench's RSC work was made up of relatively small moments, each created with exemplary care and craftsmanship. He was a member of the Company from 1963 to 95. His roles under Hall included Scroop in *Henry IV*, Gratiano in *The Merchant of Venice*, and Antonio in *The Revenger's Tragedy*. During the Nunn/Hands era, he was Page in *The Merry Wives of Windsor*, Henry IV in *When Thou Art King*, Norfolk in *Henry VIII*, Aguecheek in John Barton's *Twelfth Night*, Pistol in *Henry V*, Cymbeline, and Mr Cutler in *Nicholas Nickleby*. For Adrian Noble, Dench played the Old Shepherd in *The Winter's Tale* and Montague in *Romeo and Juliet*. With his deep voice and splendid snow-white beard, Griffith Jones was one of the RSC's most recognisable members, and something of a figurehead. During a former life he had been a dark, clean-shaven movie actor. He joined the RSC in 1975, when he was around sixty-five, and was ever-present until the end of the century. His contributions included Glendower in Terry Hands's *Henry IV*, the 1975 and 76 Other Place seasons (the Ghost in Buzz Goodbody's *Hamlet*, Duncan in Trevor Nunn's *Macbeth*), the first small-scale tour (Chebutykin in *Three Sisters*), Tim Linkinwater in *Nicholas Nickleby*, Abhorson in Adrian Noble's *Measure for Measure*, and Priam in Sam Mendes's *Troilus and Cressida*.

Barbara Jefford, one of the major players produced by Stratford during the 1950s, finally returned in 1989. She played Volumnia in *Coriolanus* for Terry Hands (1989) and the Countess in *All's Well That Ends Well* for Peter Hall (Swan, 1992).

Page 160: Ian McKellen, Francesca Annis and Trevor Nunn photographed in Stratford, March 1976.
Photograph: Evening Standard / Hulton Archive, Getty Images.

Page 161: *Romeo and Juliet* by Shakespeare, RST, 1976.
Production: Trevor Nunn. Design: John Napier.
Francesca Annis (Juliet). Photograph by Donald Cooper / Alamy.

Page 164-65: *Macbeth* by Shakespeare,
RST, 1988. Miles Anderson (Macbeth),
Amanda Root (Lady Macbeth). Production:
Adrian Noble. Design: Bob Crowley.
Photograph by Geraint Lewis / Alamy.

5

Adrian Noble

1   Background

The task of leading the RSC into a new decade fell to the most talented director of the younger generation, Adrian Noble. Adrian Noble's original, visually compelling productions of the classics had dominated the RSC's main stage since 1982. At a time when most directors, confronted by the size of the RST, sought refuge in permanent sets, Noble kept the stage bare and open to the back wall. Stark but striking scenography, the metaphorical use of objects and colour, and the fluent elision of scenes, made his work highly distinctive.

Noble was educated at Bristol University and the Drama Centre, London, and began his career working in community theatre in Birmingham. He came to notice at the Bristol Old Vic, directing Brecht's *Man is Man* (1976) and *Ubu Rex* (1977), Shakespeare's *Titus Andronicus* (1978) and *Timon of Athens* (1979), Arthur Miller's *A View from the Bridge* (1978), Middleton and Rowley's *The Changeling* (1978), Congreve's *Love for Love* (1979), and Farquhar's *The Recruiting Officer* (1979).

At the RSC, Noble started as an assistant director but was brought into the directorial team following the success of his Manchester Royal Exchange production of *The Duchess of Malfi* (1980), starring Helen Mirren and Bob Hoskins. He directed two acclaimed productions in the Other Place, Ostrovsky's *The Forest* and Ibsen's *A Doll's House*, and then, in 1982, his first main house production, a *King Lear* (starring Michael Gambon) that gripped the imagination from its very first image. 'Adrian Noble's astonishing production [is] much the best since Peter Brook's,' wrote Michael

Billington in *The Guardian*:

> The heart of this production lies in Noble's ability to mix stark tragedy with grotesque comedy: a link that is forged in the indelible opening image of the Fool and Cordelia squatting on Lear's throne, at the centre of a grey-walled courtyard reeking of tyranny, with their necks bound at opposite ends of a taut halter. As the lights go up, you realise that they are simply playing some prankish game. But the image instantly binds together the play's two out-spoken truth-tellers and the strangeness of a world in which cruelty and comedy exist side by side.[163]

The idea that Antony Sher's deformed, chalk-faced Fool was Lear's agonised conscience was carried through to a startling conclusion: Lear accidentally stabbed the Fool to death, a moment of madness but also of release. The play's fixation on the coexistence of sanity and madness was expressed by juxtapositions: one moment Lear was terrorising his courtiers, the next he was at the footlights, under a spotlight, performing a parody of a Vaudeville routine with the Fool. The stage was bare and stark, as it should be as desolation takes hold. The world created by Noble was both logical and strange.

The expression of ideas in visual terms was a common factor in his work for the RSC. *Measure for Measure* (1983) featured 18th century clothes and a beautiful cyclorama, but also a prison wall, modern lamps and an electric chair; *Henry V* (1984) magnificent tableaux of banners and light juxtaposed with images showing the realism of war (soldiers huddled together beneath tarpaulin in driving rain); and *Macbeth* (1986), starring Jonathan Pryce and Sinéad Cusack, the recurring motif of small children, a black mass for the witches and a black set which gradually contracted until long spears pierced the walls. *Macbeth* and *As You Like It* (1985) – modern-dress, parachute silk, an Arden that in all respects but colour mirrored the court – showed Noble's preoccupation with metaphors and dreams.

The Plantagenets (1988), a trilogy drawn from the *Henry VI* plays and *Richard III*, was more traditionally conceived, but the visual storytelling was unmistakably the work of the Adrian Noble/Bob

Crowley partnership. Towards the end of the second play the white floor cloth, by now smeared with blood like a butcher's apron, was lifted to hang as a backcloth against which the shadow of Anton Lesser's Richard edged towards Ralph Fiennes's Henry, imprisoned in a cage that rose up to the flies. The second play closed with a blackout following Richard's triumphant cry of 'Now'. The third opened with a sudden lights-up. From the top of a table Richard began 'Now is the winter...' as a public speech, only to jump down to address the audience, the other characters frozen in time.

As members of the RSC's board were about to consider applications to succeed Terry Hands as artistic director, Noble directed John Wood and Joanne Pearce in a rare production of Ibsen's *The Master Builder* at the Barbican (September 1989). Michael Billington called the production the 'theatrical event of the year'. Irving Wardle of *The Times* and Michael Coveney of *The Financial Times* thought it was 'magnificent'. For Jim Hiley, writing in *The Listener*, 'Noble combines a rare, televisual intimacy with the most resonant amplification of Ibsen's themes', continuing: 'Each act is sparsely furnished before a vast, sloping roof, which collapses with the master builder's demise to reveal a bleak, pygmy town. The designer is Richard Hudson, but you can only think of this moment as a characteristic *coup de théâtre* from Adrian Noble.' Michael Ratcliffe of *The Observer* observed: 'In most metropolitan European theatres Adrian Noble's breathtaking production [...] would be cherished in the repertory for months, if not years.'

For all the production's undoubted quality, members of the board may have wondered whether the critics were trying to influence their decision.

Opposite: *King Lear* by Shakespeare, RST, 1982. Michael Gambon (Lear), Antony Sher (The Fool). Production: Adrian Noble. Design: Bob Crowley. Photograph by Donald Cooper / Alamy.

2 The 1990s

Few people were surprised when Adrian Noble was appointed to succeed Terry Hands as artistic director. He had been the clear favourite for some time. Perhaps inevitably, the approval of many of the theatre critics at the time of *The Master Builder* would not be maintained once Noble was in the hot seat, making decisions. The aggressively judgemental approach adopted by sections of the press when writing about the RSC during the Nunn/Hands era would continue.

The selection panel was chaired by Geoffrey Cass and included Hands, Stanley Wells, Clive Priestley and Dennis Flower. Noble's appointment continued the Stratford tradition of promoting from within. Terry Hands, understanding better than anyone the stresses of a role that demanded fifteen-hour days, year in, year out, wisely advocated joint artistic directors. There was never any public suggestion that Hands might continue alongside Noble, with Noble moving gradually to the chief executive role, but this would have been the ideal strategy. Noble preferred to work with a deputy (Michael Attenborough, an outsider, was appointed), and the RSC's two senior administrators, Genista McIntosh, as associate producer, and David Brierley, as general manager. Genista McIntosh withdrew before the new team had taken charge (she joined Richard Eyre at the National Theatre, and would later find herself at the centre of even greater controversy at the Royal Opera House). She wasn't replaced, but Noble brought in two producers, Lynda Farran and Nicky Pallot, to oversee productions and to form new links between acting companies and management.

The associate directors departed. This was surprising because it had been assumed that an insider like Noble would value continuity. Accusations that the associates had been pushed out were denied by those individuals who chose to comment. At the very least it seems that Noble wanted total freedom to make his mark on the Company.¹⁶⁴ He brought in several talented newcomers to direct productions during his first season, 1991, with mixed results.¹⁶⁵ He would need time to build a new team of associates. Trevor Nunn returned to open the new Other Place.

Noble initially focused on the classical repertory. Some commentators misread this as a rejection of new work. Like Trevor Nunn in 1969, Noble was concentrating on first principles and needed time to find and commission work of sufficient merit and originality. So much of post-war British drama and theatre had been parochial, polemical, earnest and theatrically dull. At the RSC, beginning in the 1980s, it was possible to detect a different attitude, a belief in a theatre of ideas, style and sensuality. Noble certainly featured more French, German, Austrian and Italian writers (Molière, Marivaux, Beckett, Koltès, Yasmina Reza, Schiller, Goethe, Kleist, Büchner, Wedekind, Botho Strauss, Goldoni, Verga) than any of his predecessors. If Noble wasn't able to galvanise the Company in the manner of Peter Hall or Trevor Nunn, his first years in charge were generally considered to be successful. Michael Billington wrote in 1993: 'The Royal Shakespeare Company has discovered a new sense of purpose – and stopped doing bad musicals – under its tow-haired maestro, Adrian Noble.'¹⁶⁶

As a director Noble was working at the height of his powers, creating, in the first three years of his directorship, important work – the two parts of *Henry IV*, the three Oedipus plays of Sophocles (*The Thebans*), *The Winter's Tale*, *Hamlet*, and *King Lear*. In the *Henries* (1991) the décor was colour-coded, grey for the court, red for the tavern. Gads Hill was represented by misty blue light and a corpse tied to a post. One example of the production's cinematic style: as Henry's corpse was carried from his death chamber the scene 'dissolved' into Shallow's orchard (beekeepers like ghosts). Michael Billington thought that the production marked a 'radical new approach to the staging of Shakespeare's Histories. [...] [Noble] combines visual stylisation with psychological realism.'¹⁶⁷ *The Winter's Tale* (1992) featured a gauze cube of travelling clouds, in which figures were conjured, and the recurrent use of coloured balloons. The play's contrasts were achieved with rapid transitions, and the overall theme of redemption was movingly realised. *Hamlet* (1992), set in the early 20th century with references to Ibsen and

Munch, found visual equivalents for the themes of decay and death. The ash-grey set of the last act – a grey sheet covered the stage until Ophelia (Joanne Pearce)[168] pulled it away to reveal decayed funeral wreaths and the upright piano she had played in act one – provided an atmosphere of loss and sterility. Hamlet met the players at a railway station – a reference to RSC history, since every spring from 1886 to 1919 Stratford people met Frank Benson's company at the station. The early performances ended with Hamlet and the other victims of the play forming a group at the rear of the stage, a tableau that suggested a sepia photograph of long-dead figures, but this idea was abandoned by the time of the press night. Noble's second version of *King Lear* (1993) was more direct, less radical, than the 1982 production. A sense of humankind's insignificance in the cosmos was conveyed by the massive planetary symbol that dominated the play, spectacularly fracturing to release a column of sand after Gloucester's blinding. Vertical rain during the storm, graphic acts of violence throughout. The interpretation complemented the haunted and haunting performance, his last, of Robert Stephens.

A Midsummer Night's Dream (1994) transformed objects into metaphors (a 'forest' of swaying light bulbs, umbrellas, doors without rooms) and used electric colours. It was a dazzling variation on Peter Brook's iconic production, but the cast of talented young actors found it difficult to flesh out their characters. *Romeo and Juliet* (1995) was dark and original, but the 19th century setting was a mixed blessing. *Cymbeline* (1997) was staged as both a fable and a dream: a billowing white cloth rose and fell within a wide sky-blue box. *Twelfth Night* (1997) lacked the cinematic flow usually associated with Noble and was not a success. Its originality lay in its rejection of autumnal melancholy for a brightly-coloured setting in which cruelty and pain were not hidden beneath nostalgia. The garish costumes fixed the actors within predictable archetypes. *The Tempest* (1998) was a return to form: designer Anthony Ward and lighting designer Howard Harrison conjured thunder-green skies and an atmosphere of dislocation and wonder. On a bare stage of shingle the only object was a huge white conch shell out of which Robert Glenister's mud-black Caliban emerged. The *mise en scène* was remarkable and true to Shakespeare's text, and David Calder was a superb Prospero, but Noble was no longer popular with the critics and the reviews were at best indifferent. In the Swan, Noble delivered intimate productions of Chekhov, Ibsen and T.S. Eliot.

Noble attempted to make the Barbican a success with the public and his actors by scheduling prestigious revivals, including the Branagh *Hamlet*, and by organising a festival called *Everyone's Shakespeare*, but attitudes remained stubbornly negative. The Barbican's strengths were undervalued by Noble. In 1995 he decided that the RSC should withdraw from the Barbican for six months of the year. He established a second provincial residency, in Plymouth. This change came into operation in 1997. In 1996, Noble decided to run the Stratford season from autumn to autumn, along European lines. From 1999 the Stratford year was divided between winter and summer seasons.

During the first years of Noble's directorship, the quality of the work in the main house was variable. The young Sam Mendes matched Noble with his productions of *The Alchemist* in the Swan (1991), *Richard III*, starring Simon Russell Beale, at the Other Place (1992), and *The Tempest*, starring Alec McCowen and Beale, in the main house (1993), and surely would have kept working at Stratford if he hadn't taken charge of the Warehouse in London. Terry Hands returned to mount a superb account of Marlowe's *Tamburlaine the Great* in the Swan, but subsequently moved to Wales to run Theatr Clwyd. By 1996, Noble had established an in-house team of associate directors – Michael Attenborough, Katie Mitchell, Steven Pimlott, Michael Boyd and Gregory Doran. Attenborough, previously best-known as an interpreter of new plays, directed fine productions of *Romeo and Juliet* in the Swan (1997) and *Othello* in the main house (1999). Steven Pimlott directed T.S. Eliot's *Murder in the Cathedral* (1993) and Tennessee Williams's *Camino Real* (1997) in the Swan, as well as *Richard II* (2000) at the Other Place, and *Hamlet* (2001) in the main house. Gregory Doran revalued Shakespeare's *Henry VIII* (1996) and directed Antony Sher in *The Winter's Tale* (1998) and Sher and Harriet Walter in *Macbeth* (1999). Katie Mitchell, working in the studios, created hauntingly enigmatic and austere productions of *A Woman Killed With Kindness* (1991), Ibsen's *Ghosts* (1993), Strindberg's *Easter* (1995) and Chekhov's *Uncle Vanya* (1998). Michael Boyd, a master of Jacobean horror, directed John Ford's *The Broken Heart*

(1996), John Kyd's *The Spanish Tragedy* (1997) and confirmed his stature with the close-up despair of the *Henry VI* plays (2000). His main house *A Midsummer Night's Dream* (1999) was a worthy successor to Noble's 1994 production.

The formation of the new team was a clear achievement, allowing the creative management of the RSC to be shared (by 2000 the structures were strong enough for Noble to spend part of the year in Aix-en-Provence, directing Monteverdi's *Le retour d'Ulysse dans sa patrie*, a great success). In 1997 Noble announced plans to develop the site of the old Collins's Music Hall in Islington into a new London home for the RSC. A six hundred seat theatre, designed by Nicholas Thompson and Julian Middleton of Renton Howard Wood Levin Partnership, would be shared by the RSC (six months of the year), the Manchester Royal Exchange (three months) and Out of Joint and other companies (three months). Compressed air technology would allow the auditorium and stage to be configured to suit the production, meaning that the RSC would, at last, own a London theatre that could mirror the Swan. The project team asked the lottery commission to contribute £14 million of the £18 million total. The lottery commission turned down the bid, but agreed to part-finance the redevelopment of the RST.[169]

Dissatisfaction with the Stratford main house had increased during the 1990s. Too few directors could master the space, and actors compared it unfavourably with the Swan.[170] The balcony seats were too far from the stage. By 2000 it was clear that the RSC had a preference for the most radical solution – a new building designed by the Dutch architect Erick van Egeraat. The Arts Council contributed £755,140 towards the cost of a feasibility study in May 2000 (donations from individuals and local government[171] completed the £3.3 million total), and subsequently awarded the RSC £50 million of lottery money. This left the Company with the task of raising the same amount in the private sector: nearly £30 million had been promised by 2000. The feasibility study, carried out in 2001, produced a business plan and a scheme for the surrounding roads and public places. The RSC consulted its staff, audience and the local community.

In the meantime new attempts were made to improve the actor-audience relationship. In 1999 the stage was re-designed to become a semi-circular disk stretching into the stalls. It worked, but was cautious, a denial of the full depth of the stage and that great back wall. In 2001 the forestage was brought further forward and extended across the whole width of the auditorium (fifty feet) to widen the acting area in front of the proscenium. Both the stage and auditorium (designed by Alison Chitty) were painted the same shade of grey. 2002 saw the return of the standard configuration.

During the 1990s Noble's RSC remained the Company he'd inherited. Peter Hall returned in 1992 and 1995 (his first main stage production since 1967), and directed John Barton's *Tantalus* in 2000. Barton himself directed a fine *Peer Gynt* in 1994, and his verse workshops (based on Shakespeare's sonnets) once more became an integral part of RSC life in Stratford. In this way the RSC was moving forward while acknowledging the past. The complete history play cycle (2000/01)[172] and the Other Place season of new plays by Peter Whelan, Martin McDonagh and David Edgar (2001) received particular acclaim. Given the changing priorities of actors in the 1990s, resulting from increased opportunities, particularly on television, Noble was successful in persuading both RSC veterans and talented newcomers to make the financial and career sacrifices that working for a year at a time in Stratford entailed.

Hamlet by Shakespeare, Barbican, 1992. Rob Edwards (Horatio), Kenneth Branagh (Hamlet). Production: Adrian Noble. Design: Bob Crowley. Photograph by Richard Baker / Getty Images. Previous page: *Uncle Vanya* by Chekhov, Young Vic, 1998. Linus Roache (Astrov), Anastasia Hille (Yelena). Production: Katie Mitchell. Design: Vicki Mortimer. Photograph by Geraint Lewis / Alamy.

3 Innovation and Controversy

In May 2001 Adrian Noble formally announced details of the scheme to build a new Royal Shakespeare Theatre, along with a radical plan to change how the RSC operated. The plan involved the redevelopment of Stratford (creating a new studio theatre and a training academy for young actors), the withdrawal from the Barbican (leaving the RSC without a London home, but with more flexibility to open new productions in appropriate performing spaces), and the introduction of a structure based on short contracts and one-off productions (to suit the working lives of actors, particularly the Company's senior alumni). The RSC gave these measures a collective name – Project Fleet. At the time of the announcement, the theatre critics expressed little affection for the RST.[173]

What was happening within the Company? The context is important. In 1996 David Brierley, the RSC's highly respected general manager, retired after nearly thirty years of careful stewardship. After a long search, an executive from industry, with no theatre experience, was recruited to the new position of managing director.[174] Then, in 2000, Geoffrey Cass stepped down as chairman. He was succeeded by a former chairman of Nat West bank, Lord Alexander. The board was becoming dominated by business people, and the executive began to adopt policies, practices and jargon from the business world (company cars for managers; deals with agents to exploit the RSC 'brand'; contracts with gagging orders). While this business-oriented approach did not directly interfere with artistic policy, it had the damaging consequence of alienating many members of staff. The RSC had always portrayed itself as a community of artists, craftspeople and others. Members of staff were encouraged to feel that they belonged in the Company. Suddenly their cottage industry was being run like the arts division of a multinational conglomerate. As for Noble, he had been at the head of the Company for ten years, and, with the end of his directorship in sight, was in a hurry to realise his vision for the Company.

An anonymous RSC insider told *The Observer* that the policies of Project Fleet were hastily assembled during a managers' away day in January 2001; that the board sanctioned them without seeing a detailed business plan; and that the associate directors were split down the middle, with Michael Boyd and Gregory Doran largely in favour and Steven Pimlott and Michael Attenborough largely against.[175] It may be unwise to believe the account of an anonymous source. Pimlott supported the need for change,[176] and the suggestion that the ideas had not been considered in advance is not believable. Their implementation, though, was so rushed that the practical aspects and consequences were not thought through. Unfortunately, Cass and Brierley weren't in post to counsel caution.

Following a meeting during which Noble explained the changes to the Company's advisory directors, Terry Hands quietly stepped down: he didn't think that the plans were 'financially or artistically viable'.[177] The replacement of the RST proved the controversial tenet of Project Fleet, in that it received most of the adverse publicity. If a majority of actors disliked the RST, those who chose to speak out – Judi Dench, Donald Sinden ('There's nothing wrong with the theatre'), Michael Gambon ('It's preposterous') and Michael Pennington[178] – argued for the status quo. Noble's plan to modernise Stratford was also challenged by a local protest group called HOOT (or 'Hands Off Our Theatre') and in the arts sections of the broadsheets. However, it was Noble's decision to make the RSC homeless in London and to divide the ensemble into temporary units that caused the real concern. To what extent would the RSC remain a genuine company? As opposition to the changes grew, Noble defended his ideas.[179] In an article in *The Guardian* he wrote:

> The most potent lesson I have learned after a decade at the Royal Shakespeare Company is that to keep what happens on the stage fresh, you simply cannot stand still. Most people's fears have focused on [...] a mistaken belief that the repertoire ensemble is being dismantled [...]. The truth is, we have no intention of abandoning [this]. Next year, three companies of actors will

each present very different, but equally authentic versions of the repertoire ensemble.[180]

Noble had persuaded himself that he could remove the factors that made the RSC unique without wrecking the RSC; that by splitting the troupe into separate ensembles he would strengthen the ensemble. An ensemble is any group of actors working on one or more productions. This is not the same as a single troupe performing a repertory season.

Noble coped with a Jeremy Paxman grilling on BBC Two's *Newsnight*,[181] and successfully argued the Company's case when called to appear before the Culture, Media and Sport Select Committee of MPs. Noble took Sinéad Cusack (an inspired choice), Chris Foy and Jonathan Pope (Redevelopment Director) to face the committee. The MPs' comments were instructive: Gerald Kaufman couldn't think of an arts organisation that was more important; Chris Bryant called the RST 'hideous' and told Noble to pull it down; the prescient Michael Fabricant worried that pressure groups such as the Theatre Trust would force the RSC into keeping parts of the existing building and prevent it from going ahead with the demolition and rebuilding that he supported. The select committee supported the plans for Stratford,[182] as did the Arts Council of England.

If Noble had political encouragement, his loss of support within the Company was compounded by his decision to direct *Chitty Chitty Bang Bang* in the West End. Criticism, much of it personal and vitriolic, snowballed, and when Noble returned to work after the *Chitty* opening in March 2002 it seems that he realised that his position was untenable: a majority of the staff were irrevocably against him; some members of the board of governors had suddenly lost their nerve. A letter of concern written by Judi Dench, supporting a submission to the RSC's board from the Rudolf Kempe Society, was decisively damaging to Noble. 'I applaud your submission to the RSC governors and you have my wholehearted support,' Judi Dench wrote. 'I am deeply worried about what is happening, as I know are so many people in the profession.' The letter was leaked to the editor of *The Stage*, who published details on 18 April.[183] A week later, on 24 April, Noble, under intense pressure, announced that he would step down at the end of his contract in March 2003.

Noble tried to do too much too quickly. The RSC should have stayed at the Barbican and looked for a new London theatre. Noble tried his best with the Collins's Music Hall scheme but was unable to secure public money. The scheme wasn't grand enough or exciting enough. One senses that a solution can be found somewhere in London. The Odéon Theatre in Paris converted an old warehouse to create the Ateliers Berthier.

The Stratford redevelopment scheme was not given a fair hearing. When Noble used the term 'theatre village' to convey the scale and ambition of the plan, his detractors in the press decided he wanted to turn Stratford into a kind of theme park (Éric Ruf, director of the Comédie-Française, used the similar term 'cité du théâtre' when outlining, in 2016, his theatre's plan for a new complex in northern Paris – the French press didn't object). As a result, a long-held plan to create a new main house at Stratford (dating from the time of Peter Hall), a new flexible TOP and a base for a training academy was never seriously debated in the public forum of the press. Within the RSC, the staffing implications were mismanaged. The harsh impact of the reforms on individual employees created a division between those managers in favour of the changes and everyone else. Most serious of all, by abandoning its permanent London home and the long Stratford repertory season the RSC was giving up its unique position within the British theatre.

The Academy was established in the summer of 2002. Sixteen drama school graduates came together under Declan Donnellan's direction. The ten-week training at the Other Place centred on the creation of a production of *King Lear*, which played at the Swan and the Young Vic before touring to Spain, Italy and France (Théâtre de la Manufacture, Nancy). Noble planned a permanent school that would feed actors into the RSC's core ensemble. The Academy folded on his departure.

The work delivered by the changes was of a good quality. The productions of Shakespeare's late romances at the Roundhouse, the RSC's first post-Barbican shows, were compelling, and the Jacobean season at the Swan was acclaimed. This last was a personal success for Gregory Doran, who formed a crack ensemble of young actors to perform five works – *Edward III* (by Shakespeare and others), *Eastward Ho!* (by Jonson, Marston and Chapman), *The Roman Actor* (by Massinger), *The Island Princess* (by Fletcher) and *The Malcontent* (by Marston). In an attempt to replicate the fluent working methods of the Jacobean stage (and to get the full repertoire on the stage quickly), Doran asked his actors and fellow directors to create a production after only three weeks of rehearsal. Born under the vitriolic criticism of the reforms and threatened in its first weeks of rehearsal by the illness of one director[184] and the last-minute resignation of another,[185] Doran's vibrant project defied expectations.

For most of his twelve years at the helm, Adrian Noble had largely maintained the RSC of Hall and Brook, Nunn and Hands. The changes of 1999 and 2001 began the process that would see the RSC transform into a new shape. At the gathering of RSC artistic directors that marked the closure of the Royal Shakespeare Theatre, in 2007, Noble wryly observed that he didn't know whether he should sit beside Nunn and Hands or his successor Michael Boyd. He understood the significance of the changes he had made in 2001, and one suspects regretted them.

Macbeth by Shakespeare, Swan Theatre, 1999. Ken Bones (Banquo), Harriet Walter, Antony Sher. Production: Gregory Doran. Photograph by Geraint Lewis / Alamy.

4 Noble's RSC: Some Representative Actors

Adrian Noble built his first seasons around the figure of Robert Stephens. Noble had never forgotten seeing Stephens in *The Royal Hunt of the Sun* during his schooldays in Chichester. Previous attempts to lure Stephens to the RSC, both during his National Theatre heyday and after, had failed, but he had been absent from the stage, and out of the spotlight, for some years and was ready to return to classical roles. His Falstaff in the two parts of *Henry IV* was a cagey, predatory and mean old operator – the performance seemed to encapsulate Dylan Thomas's 'rage, rage against the dying of the light'. Every performance was subtly different, an improvisation within the margins of the play. Stephens's distinctive, alliterative delivery of the lines highlighted key phrases ('I am old,

old', 'If I had a thousand sons'). He spoke the speech on honour ('...honour is a mere scutcheon') leaning against the proscenium wall, spitting out the obscure final word to give it meaning. The title role in *King Lear* followed. Stephens was seriously ill, but it was a masterly performance. Speaking the line 'When we are born we cry that we are come to this great stage of fools... This is a good block...' he slapped the Stratford stage with the palm of his hand as though it represented all the theatres of his life.

Around Stephens, Noble placed a number of actors who had significant RSC histories. David Bradley had been a member for over ten years. He played Shallow in the second part of *Henry IV* and Gloucester in *King Lear*, and Polonius in the Branagh *Hamlet*. He made Shallow vain and manipulative, while delivering the comedy, and looked for good motives in Polonius, a highly original reading. David Calder first appeared at the RSC in 1971/72, and during the 1980s played York in *The Plantagenets*. Following his charismatic Kent in the Stephens *King Lear*, he played a contemporary Shylock, Sir Toby Belch in *Twelfth Night* and Prospero in *The Tempest*. Joanne Pearce was Doll in the second part of *Henry IV*. She was equally striking and unusual as Hilde Wangel in *The Master Builder*, Antigone in *The Thebans*, Ophelia in *Hamlet*, Rita in *Little Eyolf*, and Imogen in *Cymbeline*.

Simon Russell Beale was the great emerging talent of this period. During his first seasons with the Company, 1986-89, he had played clowns or grotesques, including the Young Shepherd in *The Winter's Tale* and three Restoration fops (he discovered in Sir Fopling Flutter an inner life of loneliness and pain). From 1990 he came into his own in all genres: Thersites in *Troilus and Cressida*, Navarre in *Love's Labour's Lost*, Marlowe's Edward II, Konstantin in *The Seagull*, Richard III, Ariel to Alec McCowen's Prospero, Oswald in *Ghosts*, and Edgar in *King Lear*.

No RSC actor of the period had a stronger stage personality than Richard McCabe. Constantly unpredictable, he made a virtue out of nonchalance. His 'Just William' Puck – school blazer and shorts, wings sticking out of his shoulders – was a remarkable reinvention of a familiar role: insolent, cocky, finding new verbal jokes in the text. During the Noble years he played Autolycus in *The Winter's Tale*, Marlowe in Peter Whelan's *The School of Night*, Flamineo in

The White Devil, Thersites in *Troilus and Cressida*, and Iago.

Amanda Harris came to the RSC from Cheek-By-Jowl in 1986. She played Emilia in *The Two Noble Kinsmen*, a bossy upper-class Hermia in *A Midsummer Night's Dream*, Ruby in Peter Flannery's *Singer*, and Virgilia in *Coriolanus*. Under Noble, she was a wounded Kate, amazed to find love, in *The Taming of the Shrew*, Penelope in Derek Walcott's version of *The Odyssey*, and Cecily in Stoppard's *Travesties*.

For years it looked as if David Troughton would be best known as a television actor. His career changed when he joined the RSC in 1982. He began with the Porter in *Macbeth* and for some years comedic roles dominated, reflecting his ability as a true if idiosyncratic clown. He played Conrade in *Much Ado About Nothing*, the clown in the Michael Gambon/Helen Mirren *Antony and Cleopatra*, the Essex idiot Blunt, robbed and left naked by a whore, in *The Rover*, and Cob in *Every Man in His Humour*. The climax of this first phase came in 1989 with his performance as Bottom in John Caird's production of *A Midsummer Night's Dream*, a masterpiece of pure comedy. He now joined the first division of classical actors: Hector in *Troilus and Cressida*, Kent in the John Wood *King Lear*, Holofernes in *Love's Labour's Lost*, Zanetto/Tonino in Goldoni's *The Venetian Twins*, Caliban in *The Tempest*, Richard III, Lopakhin in *The Cherry Orchard*, and Bolingbroke/Henry IV.

Alex Jennings excelled at comedic, character and leading dramatic roles. His rise to prominence owed much to Nicholas Hytner, who cast him as Lucio in *Measure for Measure* at the RSC in 1987. Jennings was an unusual Richard II, strong and sardonic, in Ron Daniels's production, an inspired Peer Gynt, Oberon in *A Midsummer Night's Dream*, Angelo in *Measure for Measure*, Benedick, and Hamlet.

New to the RSC was the talented, saturnine Dubliner Finbar Lynch, who, in 1991, played Surly in *The Alchemist* and the predatory Wendoll in Thomas Heywood's *A Woman Killed With Kindness*. He progressed to Mark Antony in *Julius Caesar*, Tullus Aufidius in *Coriolanus*, Lucio in *Measure for Measure*, and Puck to Jennings's Oberon. His Puck was sly, sarcastic and not a little sadistic. Another newcomer was Toby Stephens, Coriolanus to Lynch's Aufidius. Stephens had an arrogance on stage that made him the perfect actor for Coriolanus, but also for Bertram in *All's Well That Ends Well* and Lysander in *A Midsummer Night's Dream*. He would later, during the Boyd years, play Hamlet.

Emma Fielding played opposite Stephens as a touching Hermia in *The Dream*. Slight and dark-eyed, with an expressive, instantly recognisable voice, she had made her name as Thomasina in Tom Stoppard's *Arcadia* at the National in 1993. At the RSC, as well as Hermia, she played the perfect Viola in an otherwise bland *Twelfth Night*, the doomed Penthea, giving up on Iain Glen and life, in John Ford's *The Broken Heart*, Lady Teazle in *The School for Scandal*, Isabella in *Measure for Measure*, and Imogen in *Cymbeline*.

Among the other newcomers to the RSC who gave notable performances during the Noble years were Owen Teale (Hotspur, Edmund in *King Lear*), Ian Hughes (Fortinbras in *Hamlet*, the Fool in *King Lear*, Arlecchino in *The Venetian Twins*), Guy Henry (Cloten in *Cymbeline*, King John, Malvolio), Saskia Reeves (Annabella in *Tis Pity She's a Whore*, Anne in *A Woman Killed With Kindness*), Desmond Barrit (Trinculo in *The Tempest*, Malvolio, Bottom, Falstaff), Samantha Bond (Hermione in *The Winter's Tale*, Rosalind), Paul Jesson (Prospero, Henry VIII), Jeremy Northam (Horner in *The Country Wife*, Berowne in *Love's Labour's Lost*), Alexandra Gilbreath (Regina in *Ghosts*, Hermione in *The Winter's Tale*, Rosalind, Kate in *The Shrew*), Lucy Whybrow (Eleanora in Strindberg's *Easter*, Juliet), Kate Duchêne (Alithea in *The Country Wife*, Varya in *The Cherry Orchard*), Iain Glen (Henry V), Monica Dolan (Katherine in *Henry V*, Kate in *The Shrew*), Olivia Williams (*Peer Gynt*, Calantha in *The Broken Heart*), David Tennant (Touchstone, Romeo), Robert Glenister (Alfred in *Little Eyolf*, Caliban in *The Tempest*), Damian Lewis (Borghejm in *Little Eyolf*, Posthumus in *Cymbeline*), Ray Fearon (Romeo, Othello, Pericles), Zoë Waites (Juliet, Desdemona, Viola), Claire Cox (Beatrice in *A Servant to Two Masters*, Portia in *Julius Caesar*), John Light (Konstantin in *The Seagull*), and Anna Madeley (Ilse in Peter Whelan's *A Russian in the Woods*, Domitia in *The Roman Actor*, Maria in *The Malcontent*).

Noble brought back into the RSC some veterans from the Hall and Nunn eras. Back in the early 1960s, Alec McCowen played the Fool in Peter Brook's *King Lear*, and Antipholus of Syracuse in

Clifford Williams's *Comedy of Errors*. A long membership of the RSC seemed likely, but, for whatever reason, McCowen's career path led away from Stratford. He became one of the cinema's finest character actors, seemingly unassuming but a true original, admired by Joseph Losey, Alfred Hitchcock and Martin Scorsese. After thirty years away McCowen accepted Noble's invitation to play Prospero, Gaev in *The Cherry Orchard*, and Elgar in *Elgar's Rondo*.

Clifford Rose was a key player from 1960 to 69. A talented and versatile Shakespearean – Priam in *Troilus and Cressida*, Dromio of Ephesus in *The Comedy of Errors*, the Duke of Exeter in *The Wars of the Roses*, Shallow in *The Merry Wives of Windsor*, Mountjoy in *Henry V*, Nestor in *Troilus and Cressida*, Don John in *Much Ado About Nothing* – he was also a member of Peter Brook's group, appearing in *Marat/Sade* and *US*. Returning to Stratford as a white-haired senior player in 1989, he was one of the mainstays of Noble's Company, playing Scroop in the two parts of *Henry IV*, Tiresias in *The Thebans*, the Ghost in the Branagh *Hamlet*, the Second Priest in *Murder in the Cathedral*, Gonzalo in *The Tempest*, the Duke in *Othello*, and Francis Nurse in *The Crucible*.

Barry Stanton and Ian Hogg began their RSC careers within Brook's group, performing alongside Rose in *US*. Stanton went on to play first Snug and then Bottom in Brook's *A Midsummer Night's Dream*, Caliban in *The Tempest*, Oswald in Brook's film of his 1962 *King Lear*, Captain Boboyedovin in Gorky's *Enemies*, and Banquo in the Nicol Williamson *Macbeth*. Hogg was Edmund in the *King Lear* film, and starred as Coriolanus in Trevor Nunn's *The Romans*. They both re-joined the Company in the 1990s. Hogg was superb as Wolsey in *Henry VIII*, Belarius in *Cymbeline*, Capulet in *Romeo and Juliet* and Julius Caesar. Stanton was thuggish, threatening and temperamental as Stephano in *The Tempest*, Shamrayev in *The Seagull* and Sir Toby Belch in *Twelfth Night*. John Kane, a product of Saint-Denis's Studio and Brook's Puck in *The Dream*, was another celebrated returnee, playing Peter Quince, Norfolk in *Henry VIII* and the Soothsayer in *Cymbeline*.

Julian Glover was an apprentice actor at Stratford from 1957 to 59, and played the Baron in Gorky's *The Lower Depths* during the RSC's season at the Arts in 1962. In the 1970s he worked for Terry Hands, playing Medley in *The Man of Mode*, Warwick in *Henry VI* and Alonzo in *The Changeling*. Under Noble, he was outstanding as Henry IV, Friar Laurence in *Romeo and Juliet* and, reunited with Peter Hall, Cassius in *Julius Caesar*.

Philip Voss started his career at the RSC in 1960/61. Returning thirty years later, he was at last able to reveal his mastery of Shakespeare's characterisation and verse. He was cast in roles that suited his rather pedantic manner and his fruitily precise delivery of the verse, including the Lord Chief Justice in the two parts of *Henry IV*, Sir Epicure Mammon in *The Alchemist*, Theseus in *The Thebans*, Menenius in *Coriolanus*, Peter Quince in *A Midsummer Night's Dream*, and Bassanes in *The Broken Heart*. He went on to play the major roles of Ulysses in *Troilus and Cressida*, Malvolio, Shylock, and Prospero.

Jane Lapotaire played Viola in *Twelfth Night*, Sonya in *Uncle Vanya*, Rosaline in *Love's Labour's Lost*, and Piaf, a remarkable interpretation of the great singer, in Pam Gems's hit play, during the Nunn years. She was Noble's senior actress in the 1990s, playing Gertrude in the Branagh *Hamlet*, Mrs Alving in *Ghosts*, and Katherine – emphasising the pain of exile by means of accent and expression – in *Henry VIII*.

The Alchemist by Ben Jonson, Swan, 1991. Joanne Pearce (Doll), David Bradley (Subtle). Production: Sam Mendes. Design: Anthony Ward.

Previous page: *Ghosts* by Ibsen, Pit, 1994. Simon Russell Beale (Oswald), Jane Lapotaire (Mrs Alving). Production: Katie Mitchell. Design: Vicki Mortimer. Photographs by Donald Cooper / Alamy.

PART THREE

6
A New Era

Women Beware Women by Thomas Middleton, Swan Theatre, 2006. Hayley Atwell (Bianca), Tim Pigott-Smith (Duke of Florence). Production: Laurence Boswell. Design: Richard Hudson. Photograph by Geraint Lewis / Alamy.

Page 190: *Brand* by Ibsen, Swan Theatre, 2003. Ralph Fiennes (Brand), Claire Price (Agnes). Production: Adrian Noble. Design: Peter McKintosh. Photograph: PA Images / Alamy.

The Crucible by Arthur Miller, RST, 2006. Iain Glen (Proctor), Elaine Cassidy (Abigail). Production: Dominic Cooke. Design: Hildegard Bechtler. Photograph by Geraint Lewis / Alamy.

1 Semtex Boyd

In April 2003 Michael Boyd succeeded Adrian Noble as artistic director. He may have been chosen over the other inside candidate, Gregory Doran, because his production style was more original. The selection panel included Sinéad Cusack and other members of the board, and one outsider – Sir Richard Eyre. As well as Boyd and Doran, the panel considered joint applications from John Caird and Simon Russell Beale and Jonathan Kent and Ian McDiarmid. Baz Bamigboye reported in his column in the *Daily Mail* (9 August 2002) that, according to a governor, the panel was disappointed that neither Sam Mendes nor Michael Grandage had applied, and that Eyre considered Doran's productions to be bland.

For the first time in over twenty years the press gave an artistic director of the RSC some slack. This was perhaps because the RSC was no longer considered important enough to warrant the aggressively critical scrutiny that had been the case under Nunn, Hands and Noble. As a consequence, major policy decisions would be implemented without any real scrutiny.

Boyd grew up in Belfast and Edinburgh. Following his studies at Edinburgh University he trained under Anatoly Efros at the Malaya Bronnaya Theatre in Moscow (1979). For ten years he ran the Tron Theatre in Glasgow. In 1994 he made his debut at the RSC directing a production of John Ford's neglected tragedy *The Broken Heart* (Swan). Performed in period costumes, the production's formal dances were juxtaposed against music (sustained notes on the strings, composed by Boyd's regular collaborator Craig Armstrong) that didn't fit – a haunting effect that was like slow-motion in film. Ford's suffering people were movingly brought to life by a fine cast (Iain Glen, Emma Fielding, Olivia Williams). *Much Ado About Nothing* (1996) was notable for its darkness of tone. *Measure for Measure* (1998) concentrated on paranoia and danger, on personal and public breakdown. The play was set in an enclosed space until the final moments, when the full depth of the stage was revealed – the Duke and Isabella walked slowly away into this previously hidden world. In *A Midsummer Night's Dream* (1999) the forest was a laboratory of desire, sensuality and transformation. Roses bloomed from the floorboards; actors burst through trap doors. Boyd began the play in monochrome and ended it with the abandonment of an intimate dance. *Romeo and Juliet* (2000) was set, less successfully, in a similar off-white space bounded by two curved walls: there were telling ideas – sombre music (solo cello) accompanied the Mercutio/Tybalt fight – but the Romeo and Juliet of David Tennant and Alexandra Gilbreath were too mature.

Boyd was fascinated by the macabre. The murdered heroine of *The Broken Heart* was left beside a table of decaying food as the buzz of flies filled the auditorium. The victims of *The Spanish Tragedy* (1997), doomed, one by one, in purgatory, to re-live the terrible events, waited silently behind a blood-red curtain. Similarly, the ghosts of Mercutio and Tybalt witnessed the final scenes of *Romeo and Juliet*. In 2000/01 he staged the three parts of *Henry VI* and *Richard III* in the Swan to widespread acclaim.

The fact that Doran stayed on as Chief Associate Director meant that Boyd was able to spend the first year of his directorship reviewing all aspects of the RSC's operation. Vikki Heywood joined the Company as Executive Director; Laurence Boswell, Dominic Cooke and Tom Piper became associate artists. While Boyd stayed in his office, Doran produced some of the best work of his career. He continued his exploration of the work of John Fletcher by directing the same group of actors in Shakespeare's *Taming of the Shrew* and Fletcher's sequel *The Tamer Tamed* (2003). *All's Well That Ends Well* (2003) was acclaimed. But the theatre is a merciless art form. Doran's musical *Merry Wives of Windsor* (2006) was an unqualified failure, and *A Midsummer Night's Dream*, although excellent in the RST (2005), came across as forced, over-acted and visually uninspired when revived in the Courtyard. *Hamlet*, built around the popularity of David Tennant, likewise suffered from the party atmosphere in the galleries (2008). The change of mood (from torment to stoicism) that Shakespeare requires after Hamlet's return from England wasn't registered. Doran re-found his form directing Shakespeare and Fletcher's lost play *Cardenio* in the Swan (2011). The play was Doran's own deft and scholarly re-imagining, with text lifted from Lewis Theobald's *Double Falsehood*, Thomas Shelton's translation of Cervantes's *Don Quixote* and other sources.

Boyd had encouraged Noble in the drive to change how the RSC operated: he supported the departure from the Barbican and the restructuring of the Company into project-led ensembles; and his dislike of the RST was greater than Noble's own (Noble, after all, had always excelled in that space). In fact, Boyd was much more confrontational than Noble when it came to defending the changes, telling the press: 'Turning round a monster like the RSC, with its highly overdeveloped organisational memory, you are always going to upset someone, because everyone has a different idea of what its cherished values are. But without putting a little Semtex under an organisation like this you go nowhere. Subtle use of Semtex is not a bad thing.'[186] In an interview published in *The Daily Telegraph* shortly after Noble's resignation, he was more measured but no less critical, speaking of outdated working practices and of a main house that was a 'terrible place' to act in.[187] Boyd's view was that the exterior could be kept, but that the interior needed to be completely re-thought.

The question of how to re-develop the Royal Shakespeare Theatre was profound, as was the broader issue of deciding on the direction the Company should take in the 21st Century. Boyd soon revealed that he was more pragmatic than visionary. He retained Noble's summer and winter seasons, and the shorter contracts, but abandoned the scheme to build a completely new RST (and along with it a new Other Place and the RSC Academy) in favour of the conversion of the existing building. This looked like a loss of nerve. Prudence became the order of the day, with Boyd programming only the most popular plays in the main house and forming partnerships with the commercial sector to transfer them into the West End: a deal with Cameron Mackintosh, beginning in 2005/06 at the Novello Theatre, tied the RSC to the commercial sector for five risk-free years.

Boyd split the company into RST and Swan Theatre ensembles. The former was designated the 'core' company. He devoted his first main house summer season (2004) to the tragedies, and his second (2005) to the comedies. Then, for 2006/07, he organised a Shakespeare complete works festival in Stratford. Visiting companies joined the RSC in the performing of all of Shakespeare's plays. This grand project generated good publicity, but its artistic value was weakened by the inclusion of too few major productions from abroad and by the decision to split the RSC into separate ensembles. Of the thirty-eight plays in the canon, twenty-two were staged by visiting companies from Britain and abroad and sixteen by the RSC ensembles. The RSC also presented readings of Shakespeare's epic poems *The Rape of Lucrece*, *The Phoenix and the Turtle* and *Venus and Adonis* and his *Sonnets* (in collaboration with Opera North), and performed new plays by Peter Straughan, Rona Munro and Leo Butler. The highlight of the festival was the visit of the Münchner Kammerspiele. This was a historic visit, the first by a major continental European company to the Royal Shakespeare Theatre. Luk Perceval's provocative modern dress *Othello* was a deliberate deconstruction of Shakespeare's text stressing themes of isolation, nihilism, racism and the corruption of innocence. The translation lacked linguistic complexity, but the direction and the acting of Julia Jentsch and Thomas Thieme had an originality that was continually startling: it made the RSC's concurrent production of *Antony and Cleopatra* (Patrick Stewart in a wig) seem old-fashioned.

One of the RSC ensembles revived Boyd's 2000/01 productions of the three parts *Henry VI* and *Richard III*. Boyd kept the group together and staged *Richard II*, the two parts of *Henry IV* and *Henry V* in Stratford during 2007. Then, early in 2008, all eight history plays were performed in sequence at the Roundhouse in London. There is a long history of RSC directors defining their eras by staging the histories, from Anthony Quayle in the 1950s (Richard Burton, Michael Redgrave, Harry Andrews) to Hall in the 1960s (Peggy Ashcroft, Donald Sinden, Ian Holm, David Warner), from Terry Hands in the 1970s (Alan Howard, Anton Lesser, Brewster Mason, Helen Mirren) to Adrian Noble in the 1980s and 90s (Kenneth Branagh, Ralph Fiennes, Lesser, Robert Stephens). Boyd's versions of the *Henry VI* plays were first-rate, but the first four plays were less compelling, at least at the beginning of the run: some of the actors were over-stretched, and suffered in comparison with their predecessors.

When Boyd and his team finally released details of the redevelopment of the RST, it became clear that they intended to build a second Swan Theatre. They weren't concerned that the scope and style of the RSC would be limited if both theatres were configured in the same way. Although the scheme necessitated the bulldozing of the auditorium and stage of the RST, those who opposed demolition, including Judi Dench, were appeased.

2 Building a New Theatre

During the period of the closure of the RST, the Company performed in a temporary theatre called the Courtyard erected on the Other Place car park (the Other Place itself became the temporary theatre's front of house).[188] The transitional period was very well managed. The Courtyard was built in time for the Complete Works Festival. It allowed the RSC to continue to deliver a full programme during the closure and acted as a testing ground for the new RST.

Boyd was very happy with the Courtyard, and instructed the architects of the RST, Bennetts Associates, to replicate it in the new building. The decision was worrying because the work at the Courtyard, dominated by coarse acting, mediocre concepts and clumsily staged scenes, had raised serious concerns over the merits of a large indoor Jacobean-style theatre.

Small galleried playhouses like the Swan encourage an intimate, conversational style of acting. But a main house indoor theatre demands something more – images, atmosphere, and stagecraft. The playing area should be transformable. Courtyard-style theatres with their redundant high spaces and ranks of distracting spectators in every direction are clearly limiting in this respect. They tend to work as outdoor arenas under daylight, but not as indoor theatres once the audience becomes too big. Michael Boyd tried to make the Courtyard work spatially by bringing the actors down from above on ropes and trapezes: the idea was repeated too often. Perhaps most worrying of all, directors knew that if they used any part of the Courtyard's stage other than a narrow section about a third of the way down from the rear wall, a large percentage of the audience would be watching the backs of the actors' heads. Speaking about another major theatre development, the NT, back in the 1960s, Kenneth Tynan remarked:

> There is the anguished question of how far the stage should jut out into the audience. The aim is to get as many people as possible as close as possible to the stage. Geometrically, this means that the larger the prospective audience, the more you have to push the acting area out into their midst. A peninsular stage even at its best imposes on the customers a number of dire deprivations, such as staring at an actor's rear view when most you need to look at his face and hear the words he is saying. I have heard it speciously argued that a projecting stage adds a 'third dimension' to acting. What a grotesque abuse of language! *All* live acting is in three dimensions and I cannot understand how the ability to see one's fellow-spectators behind the actors materially adds to the sculptural roundness of the experience.[189]

More to the point, Peter Hall was against the thrust stage, telling *The Guardian*: 'I personally find, though it's no time to be saying it, the thrust stage difficult for complicated words. You come on down that vast diving board of a stage and address the person you're speaking to with your back to half the audience. So the moves tend to be based on whose turn it is to have a bit of text.'[190]

It is true that proscenium theatres like the old RST are unforgiving to all but the most talented directors and actors, and it looked as if the RSC's artistic director was choosing a safe option and not considering the longer term. During the last public event in the RST, Trevor Nunn, Terry Hands and Adrian Noble spoke eloquently of the theatre's importance, with Nunn explaining how Peter Hall and John Bury's decision to extend a raked stage through and beyond the proscenium created a unique RSC style. Michael Boyd, for his part, was unapologetic, dismissing the doubters by suggesting that if they preferred to sit in the dark they should go to the cinema.

The new theatre opened to the public on schedule in November 2010. The total cost of the project was £112.8 million. This included the building of the Courtyard Theatre, the creation of new rehearsal rooms in Arden Street and an administration centre in Chapel Lane, and the transformation of the RST and Swan, which lasted from April 2007 to July 2010. £113 million was a relatively modest sum. To put it in perspective, the impressive Royal Opera House redevelopment of 1997-2002 cost £178 million. The RSC was not as ambitious as the ROH. In converting the 1930s building, Bennetts Associates replaced some of the brickwork with glass panels and built a viewing tower beside the road. A new restaurant occupied the top level, behind the glass, and a new entrance area and interior walkway connected the RST and the Swan. Sadly, the architecture was uninspired and clumsy – an ugly building was made uglier by the construction, on the riverside frontage, of a huge extension that looked like a grey Portakabin (it hadn't been possible to accommodate the dressing rooms within the building).

As expected, the auditorium was a near copy of the Courtyard Theatre. Unforgivably for a new build, some of the seats gave a restricted view of the stage. The design scored in one regard only: in bringing the cheap seats much closer to the action than had been the case in the old RST. Boyd achieved his goals of making spectators as visible to each other as possible and giving them the illusion of joint ownership of the space with the performers. Celebrating his new theatre in the RSC's 2011 annual report he wrote: '[The ideal stage] should provide good opportunities for people-watching and encourage the audience to talk and wave to each other across an open stage.'[191] There may have been some sound reasons for building a thrust stage, but this was not one of them (as Tynan recognised).

Opposite: *The City Madam* by Massinger, Swan, 2011.
Pippa Nixon (Shave'em), Nathaniel Martello-White (Goldwire),
Christopher Chilton (Ding'em). Production: Dominic Hill.
Photograph by Geraint Lewis / Alamy.

3   One Company or Many?

Michael Boyd continued to split the Stratford year between summer and winter seasons and to divide the Company by theatre or project. He spoke sincerely about the importance of the ensemble, but for most of his time in charge this meant ensembles, self-contained groups of actors working on their own productions. The 2008 summer season at the Courtyard, for example, was split in the middle, with one group departing as the next arrived. Since nearly all of the well-known actors were in the second company, directed by Gregory Doran, there was a very definite sense of a first and second eleven. This kind of fragmentation was not only unnecessary; it ran counter to the sense of collective endeavour that must underpin a theatre troupe. Boyd appeared to believe in the company model as one of a number of choices within a flexible structure that, because of practical considerations, was always shifting. However, he did form long-term groups on two occasions, in 2006, to perform the histories, and in 2009. The latter company started out in Stratford in 2009, returned the following year, and then moved to the Roundhouse in London. The actors toured to New York and ended their life together opening the new RST at the beginning of 2011. They produced the finest, most sustained work of Boyd's directorship. Boyd deserved great credit here, and it was a shame that he didn't feel able to continue along the same lines. 2011 and 2012 saw a return to fragmentation.

Boyd packaged his programmes in an attempt to make them newsworthy, but the results were mixed. Laurence Boswell's Spanish Golden Age project in the Swan (2004) failed to repeat the success of his 1991 Gate Theatre Spanish season. The new work festivals of 2004/05 went by unnoticed because the plays were mediocre. 2009 saw the beginning of a new project, an exploration of contemporary writing in the countries that had been part of the Soviet Union, labelled 'Revolutions'. The season was personally important to the Moscow-trained Boyd, but the actual plays were not good enough to justify the time and resources spent on a subject of only passing interest (a wider European project, including French, German and Italian new work, would have been more prescient). Around these special projects, some of Shakespeare's most popular plays were staged too frequently. 2012 saw the fifth Stratford presentation of *Twelfth Night* since Boyd became artistic director.

The shorter contracts offered regularly by the RSC encouraged some star associate actors to return but didn't strengthen the ranks of the Company. Up-and-coming actors, realising that the RSC was not as distinctive or influential as it once was, stopped considering Stratford if they had alternative offers in London. As for the returning associates, they usually only committed to one production in Stratford with a quick London transfer guaranteed. They were rarely around for long enough to be considered integral to what Michael Boyd's ten-year directorship was about.

This didn't mean that the contribution of associate and star actors was insignificant. Toby Stephens played Hamlet for Boyd in 2005, and David Tennant followed in 2008, directed by Gregory Doran. Patrick Stewart, the most present associate during the period, was Prospero in *The Tempest*, Antony in *Antony and Cleopatra*, Claudius in the Tennant *Hamlet* and Shylock in *The Merchant of Venice*. Only Greg Hicks could match him, starring as Macbeth, Leontes in *The Winter's Tale*, Julius Caesar and King Lear. Iain Glen played John Proctor in a fine production of *The Crucible* directed by Dominic Cooke in the main house while, in the Swan, Penelope Wilton, Tim Pigott-Smith and Hayley Atwell performed a thrilling, erotically-charged version of *Women Beware Women* (2006). Most significantly, David Warner returned to Stratford after an interval of forty years to play Falstaff in the two parts of *Henry IV*. Few performances in 2007 had such meaning or emotional resonance. Doran directed Judi Dench in *All's Well That Ends Well*, Antony Sher and Amanda Harris in *Othello*, Malcolm Storry in *A Midsummer Night's Dream*, Harriet Walter in *Antony and Cleopatra*, Penny Downie and Oliver Ford Davies in *Hamlet*,

Richard McCabe and Alexandra Gilbreath in *Twelfth Night*, and Ray Fearon in *Julius Caesar*. The only former associate director to return was Trevor Nunn. He took charge of his own group during the Complete Works Festival and directed Ian McKellen and Jonathan Hyde in *King Lear* and *The Seagull*.

The RSC benefited from Boyd's decision to bring in two of the leading figures of the younger generation, David Farr and Rupert Goold. Farr directed *King Lear* (2010), *Twelfth Night* and *The Tempest* with the same actors (2012), and *Hamlet* (2013). Goold staged *Romeo and Juliet* (2010) and *The Merchant of Venice* (2011). *Romeo and Juliet* was arguably the most striking production of the period. It drew on our contemporary world of gang knifings, but also the old Europe of Don Juan and Caravaggio. Damnation waited just beneath the surface. Into this world Goold introduced a boy and a girl who could have stepped onto the stage from the audience. Goold's originality showed itself in broad strokes rather than in the analytical thinking of a Peter Hall or Trevor Nunn. Juliet's party began as a pagan dance, a rite of spring in which Juliet, as the chosen one, pirouetted wildly before being lifted and carried in a circle. The stars of the production, Sam Troughton and Mariah Gale, were comfortable enough with Shakespeare's verse to have appeared with the Company at any time in its history, as were Katy Stephens, Forbes Masson, Aislín McGuckin, Jonjo O'Neill, Susannah Fielding, Alex Hassell, Emily Taaffe, and especially Jonathan Slinger, dominating Boyd's histories as Richard II, Richard of Gloucester and Fluellen, and playing Lenny in Farr's production of Harold Pinter's *The Homecoming*. Slinger, an original and rather enigmatic presence, was his generation's Ian Holm. Another important young director, Maria Aberg, began her RSC career as an assistant director in 2006. In her provocative version of *King John* (Swan, 2012), the Bastard was a young woman, played with malignant panache by Pippa Nixon. Nixon also excelled as Dorotea in *Cardenio*, Shave'em in Massinger's *The City Madam*, Titania in *A Midsummer Night's Dream* (all 2011), Lady Anne in *Richard III* (2012), Rosalind in Aberg's lyrical *As You Like It* and Ophelia in Farr's *Hamlet* (2013). Alex Waldmann played opposite Nixon in *King John* and *As You Like It* and was her equal as a dynamic, mischievous interpreter of Shakespeare.

In October 2011, Michael Boyd announced that he would step down after ten years in charge in 2012. The decision was typical of his decisive approach to theatre management. In the second half of his time in charge, the standard of the work produced by the Company was often high, and the young actors involved had started to form their own RSC identities. Boyd, Doran, Goold, Farr and Maria Aberg were a formidable team. The timing of Boyd's departure was regrettable because it meant that the chances of his associates staying together at the RSC were slim.

King John by Shakespeare, Swan, 2012. Pippa Nixon (the Bastard), Alex Waldmann (King John). Production: Maria Aberg. Design: Naomi Dawson. Photograph by Geraint Lewis / Alamy.

The Merchant of Venice by Shakespeare, RST, 2011. Emily Plumtree (Nerissa), Susannah Fielding (Portia). Production: Rupert Goold. Design: Tom Scutt. Photograph by Geraint Lewis / Alamy.

King John by Shakespeare, Swan, 2012. Pippa Nixon (the Bastard). Production: Maria Aberg. Design: Naomi Dawson. Photograph by Geraint Lewis / Alamy.

4   Gregory Doran

By appointing Gregory Doran to succeed Michael Boyd, the RSC's board opted for continuity. However, as predicted, Boyd's associates didn't stay on.

Gregory Doran's commitment to the RSC stretched back to his days as an actor in the 1980s. Productions such as *The Island Princess* and *Cardenio* were informed by his passion for English Renaissance drama. It was expected that he would value the historic achievements of the RSC, and continue the long-established policy of bringing in the most exciting directorial talent of the day. Things turned out somewhat differently.

In 1993, during Adrian Noble's directorship, Peter Hall still believed that the RSC was the Company he founded. Remembering his late-night meeting with Fordham Flower in Leningrad in 1958, he wrote: 'The policy of the as yet unformed and unnamed Royal Shakespeare Company, its aims and ideals, were defined and finally accepted that night. They are still much the same today.'[192] During Boyd's directorship one could still detect traces of the RSC of Hall, Nunn and Hands. With every passing year, those traces become ever fainter.

Gregory Doran reduced the number of productions and didn't lengthen seasons or contracts. In the first years of his directorship, like Boyd before him, he mounted a history cycle. He directed a powerful cast – Antony Sher, David Tennant, Jasper Britton, Oliver Ford Davies, Julian Glover and Alex Hassell – in *Richard II*, the two parts of *Henry IV* and *Henry V*. Like most traditionally-costumed productions of plays that require spectacle, these Histories suffered on the RST's audience-surrounded thrust stage and would have benefited from the mystery and darkness of the former RST. *King Lear*, with Sher in the title role, came next, followed by Simon Russell Beale in *The Tempest*. The thirtieth anniversary of the opening of the Swan Theatre was marked by revivals of Shakespeare and Fletcher's *The Two Noble Kinsmen* and Aphra Behn's *The Rover*.

Among the actors brought back into the Company by Doran for short engagements were Eileen Atkins (Elizabeth Sawyer in *The Witch of Edmonton*), Henry Goodman (*Volpone*, directed by Trevor Nunn), Hugh Quarshie (Othello), Mark Lockyer (Subtle in *The Alchemist*), David Troughton (Gloucester), Graham Turner (the Fool), Lisa Dillon (Rosaline in *Love's Labour's Lost*), Alexandra Gilbreath (Angelica in *The Rover*) and Joseph Millson (Willmore in *The Rover*).

During the years 2013 to 2020, Doran leased the Barbican Theatre for short seasons of transfers but was not able to re-establish the RSC as an important London theatre. He did not establish a new team of talented associates or manage to bring in a figure of real stature. Too many of the productions of classical texts directed by the newcomers lacked good stagecraft, let alone lucidity or true originality. This could not have been predicted when Doran was appointed. He was the first artistic director to run the RSC without a cabinet of equals, meaning that the Company of the 2010s reflected the attitudes of one man. Peter Hall understood the importance of sharing the directorship of a great theatre with others. 'If you just follow your own personal obsessions, the theatre you run is only as good as you are,' he wrote in his *Diaries*. 'When Tony Quayle was at Stratford, George Devine at the Royal Court, and when I later was at the RSC, we all drew strength from the talents of others, talents that were allowed to develop because, in a sense, we allowed them to walk over us.'[193]

While box office receipts were good, one sensed a lack of ambition and a disregard for innovation, especially if one compared the RSC's output with that of the National, Chichester, the Almeida (run by the man Stratford lost, Rupert Goold) or the Young Vic. It was bad timing for Doran that his naturalistic staging of Arthur Miller's *Death of a Salesman* opened in the wake of Ivo van Hove's radical reinterpretation of Miller's *A View from the Bridge* at the Young Vic, a masterpiece of both direction and acting. The RSC seemed stuck in a comfort zone, while other theatres aspired to create visionary, primal, innovative theatre. The departure of the multi-talented David Farr was a blow for Stratford, particularly since Goold had already moved on. Maria Aberg followed her imaginative RSC productions of the final years of Michael Boyd's regime with a reinvention of Marlowe's *Doctor Faustus* (2016), but she was less present than one might have expected.

5 The Future: Think Big

The Royal Shakespeare Company can continue to function like a Chichester of the Midlands, or…

During the Boyd and Doran years it became evident that the RSC badly needed to re-establish an effective new play policy and to once again compete with the Royal Court and the National Theatre for the best new writing. This is unlikely to happen if the Company can't acquire its own theatre in London.

Securing a permanent home in London must be the RSC's first priority going forward. It will be a challenge, but here's how: find a vacant warehouse, secure the funding, select the right architect, and convert it into three theatres. It happens in Paris. Impossible in London? The Swan Theatre seemed impossible. The RSC should think big and find a way.

With a London home, a future artistic director will be able to rediscover the principles that underpinned the RSC under Peter Hall: a permanent company of directors and actors staging and performing both Shakespeare and new works in the creation of a production style that is simultaneously classical and modern. If the RSC is, first and foremost, a means of ensuring that Shakespearean acting and production are continually renewed while recognising the importance of language, then the company model gives the best return. It is not too late for the RSC to return to these core principles. The RSC may need to find a means of radically reconfiguring the Royal Shakespeare Theatre if it is to attract the most important directors and designers.

Once a London home has been re-established and long contracts reintroduced, it will be worth considering a step that neither Hall nor Nunn, Hands nor Noble, took, although they may have contemplated it. Make the RSC's London theatre the actors' base and unambiguously position Stratford as the RSC's prestigious summer festival. The actors would work mostly at the London base, presenting a continual repertory season, but a substantial number would play a full repertory across all three theatres in Stratford during the summer months. Productions would be created in London and not Stratford. The London theatre could either stay open all year or function along the same lines as Continental theatres, from the beginning of September to the end of June, and close (or be hired out) while the company is in Stratford. The RSC could appear in Stratford outside of the summer season, perhaps by mounting a Christmas show, but not continually. The Stratford theatres would be closed for part of the winter.

This may not be the best or right solution, but a permanent London home and the long contracts can be achieved and made to work. The Stratford Theatre and the RSC, as this narrative has shown, were built by extraordinary men, men of vision, daring and determination. To re-find the theatre they created – that will also require an extraordinary man or woman, but it will be the easier task.

Notes

[1] Phone conversation with Terry Hands, December 2019.
[2] *The Birmingham Daily Post*, 4 May 1892, p.5.
[3] Matthew Arnold, 'The French Play in London', in *The Nineteenth Century: a Monthly Review*, vol.6, no.30 (August 1879), p.242-43.
[4] Charles Flower, 'Speech', 2 November 1876, quoted in Sally Beauman, *The Royal Shakespeare Company: a History of Ten Decades* (Oxford: OUP, 1982), p.15.
[5] Frank Benson (1858-1939) was educated at New College, Oxford. He made his professional debut as a member of Henry Irving's company at the Lyceum in 1882.
[6] William Bridges-Adams (1889-1965).
[7] A small annual subsidy of £3,000 was allocated for three years.
[8] See *The Times*, 8 March 1926, p.9.
[9] Quoted in Sally Beauman, *The Royal Shakespeare Company: a History of Ten Decades*, p.93.
[10] *The Times*, 16 April 1926.
[11] Harley Granville-Barker, Letter to the Editor, *The Times*, 30 April 1929.
[12] *The Observer*, 8 January 1928.
[13] *The Guardian*, 27 March 1932.
[14] See Sally Beauman, *The Royal Shakespeare Company: a History of Ten Decades*, p.110.
[15] 'Shakespeare Memorial: New Theatre Opened', in *The Times*, 25 April 1932.
[16] Ibid.
[17] Ben Iden Payne (1881-1976). Managing Director 1935-43.
[18] Fordham Flower (1904-66) was educated at Winchester and Sandhurst.
[19] Barry Jackson (1879-1961).
[20] Quoted in Beauman, *The Royal Shakespeare Company: a History of Ten Decades*, p.171.
[21] This promise by Barry Jackson was printed in all the Rep programmes.
[22] Peter Brook, *Threads of Time: a Memoir* (London: Methuen, 1998), p.36.
[23] Barry Jackson, 'The New Idea at Stratford', *Theatre World*, April 1946.
[24] Kenneth Tynan, 'Love's Labour's Lost', in *A View of the English Stage, 1944-1965* (London: Methuen, 1984), p.35.

[25] Quoted in J.C. Trewin, *Paul Scofield* (London: Rockliff, 1956), p.45.
[26] '*Romeo and Juliet* at Stratford', *The Guardian*, 7 April 1947.
[27] 'Stratford Honours the Birthday in Sunshine: an Early Victorian Hamlet', *The Guardian*, 24 April 1948.
[28] Peter Hall, *Making an Exhibition of Myself* (London: Sinclair-Stevenson, 1993), p.134.
[29] See Ibid., p.189.
[30] *The Times*, 11 June 1948.
[31] *Threads of Time*, p.38.
[32] Anthony Quayle (1913-1989).
[33] *Shakespeare Memorial Theatre, 1948-1950: a Photographic Record* (London: Reinhardt and Evans, 1951).
[34] Anthony Quayle, *A Time to Speak* (London: Barrie & Jenkins, 1990), p.321.
[35] Anthony Quayle, 'The Theatre from Within', *Shakespeare Memorial Theatre, 1948-1950: a Photographic Record*, p.14.
[36] Quoted in David Addenbrooke, *The Royal Shakespeare Company: the Peter Hall Years* (London: William Kimber, 1974), p.19.
[37] See Quayle, *A Time to Speak*, p.322-23.
[38] Tynan, *A View of the English Stage, 1944-1965*, p.111.
[39] Anthony Quayle, 'Foreword', in J. Dover Wilson and T.C. Worsley, *Shakespeare's Histories at Stratford in 1951* (London: Max Reinhardt, 1952), p.vii.
[40] Tynan, *A View of the English Stage, 1944-1965*, p.112.
[41] Quoted in Michael Billington, 'A Misspent Youth', in Stanley Wells (ed.), *Summerfolk: Essays Celebrating Shakespeare and the Stratford Theatres* (Ebrington: Long Barn Books), p.45.
[42] Glen Byam Shaw (1904-1986).
[43] Beauman, *The Royal Shakespeare Company: a History of Ten Decades*, p.225.
[44] Ian Holm, *Acting My Life* (Corgi Books, 2006), p.53.
[45] Holm, *Acting My Life*, p.54.
[46] Glen Byam Shaw interviewed by Sally Beauman in 1979. Quoted in Ibid., p.232.
[47] Hall read English at St Catharine's College.
[48] See Peter Hall, 'Creating One of the Glories of World Theatre', *The Times*, 28 March 1985.
[49] See Richard Mangan (ed.), *Gielgud's Letters* (London: Weidenfeld and Nicolson, 2004), p.276-78.
[50] *Birmingham Post*, 14 January 1960.
[51] See Hall, *Making an Exhibition of Myself*, p.148.
[52] See Peter Hall, 'Shakespeare and the Modern Director', *Royal Shakespeare Theatre Company, 1960-1963* (London: Max Reinhardt, 1964), p.41-48.
[53] See Hall, *Making an Exhibition of Myself*, p.153-54.

54 The Aldwych Theatre was built in 1905.
55 Stephen Thorne. Quoted in Robert Sellers, *Peter O'Toole: the Definitive Biography* (Thomas Dunne Books, 2015), p.81.
56 Ibid., P.83.
57 Holm, *Acting My Life*, p.195.
58 Harold Hobson, 'Stratford's Third Effort', *The Sunday Times*, 22 May 1960.
59 Harold Hobson, 'Salacrou and Shakespeare', *The Sunday Times*, 32 July 1960.
60 Hall, *Making an Exhibition of Myself*, p.161.
61 Kenneth Tynan, 'Hall and Brook Ltd.', *The Observer*, 3 July 1957.
62 Peter Hall, 'Avoiding a Method: From a Talk Given to the Company in January, 1963', in *Crucial Years* (London: Max Reinhardt, 1963), p.16-17.
63 Addenbrooke, *The Royal Shakespeare Company: the Peter Hall Years*, p.192.
64 Kenneth Tynan would later write: 'The RSC (a directors' theatre) has not discovered one star actor in the twelve years since it was founded. When you lack actors, you need "interpretation" – to supply the bloodstream that is missing.' *The Diaries of Kenneth Tynan* (London: Bloomsbury, 2001), p.139.
65 Addenbrooke, *The Royal Shakespeare Company: the Peter Hall Years*, p.94.
66 In *Nova*. Quoted in Addenbrooke, *The Royal Shakespeare Company: the Peter Hall Years*, p.32.
67 Quoted in *Royal Shakespeare Theatre Company, 1960-1963*, p.185-86.
68 Ibid., p.186.
69 Addenbrooke, *The Royal Shakespeare Company: the Peter Hall Years*, p.125.
70 Hall, *Making an Exhibition of Myself*, p.192.
71 Ibid., p.191.
72 Ibid., p.174.
73 Holm, *Acting My Life*, p.80.
74 Ibid., p.81.
75 Hall, *Making an Exhibition of Myself*, p.175-76.
76 Holm, *Acting My Life*, p.82.
77 Bernard Levin in the *Daily Mail*, 21 August 1963.
78 Hall, *Making an Exhibition of Myself*, p.187.
79 Harold Hobson, 'The Off-beat Hamlet', *The Sunday Times*, 22 August 1965.
80 Hall, *Making an Exhibition of Myself*, p.162. I should add that, curiously, I haven't been able to identify any review or article by Hobson in *The Sunday Times* in 1960 in which he objects to the Company setting up shop at the Aldwych. This may be because of faulty metadata.
81 See Sellers, *Peter O'Toole*, p.95.
82 For a detailed telling of the process see Beauman, *The Royal Shakespeare Company: a History of Ten Decades*, p.252-65.
83 Hall, *Making an Exhibition of Myself*, p.170.

84 *The Daily Telegraph*, 14 March 1962.
85 *The Daily Telegraph*, 9 July 1962.
86 The long delay in the completion of the Barbican meant that the RSC remained at the Aldwych for twenty years.
87 Hall, *Making an Exhibition of Myself*, p.171.
88 See Michael Redgrave, *In My Mind's Eye: an Autobiography* (Coronet Books, 1984), p.130.
89 Ibid., p.135. Redgrave on *Three Sisters*: 'One day when I came to Tuschenbach's speech about migratory birds in Act Two, Michel gestured at me impatiently with his pipe-stem… "No, no, my friend. You speak as if the lines were important." "Isn't that what an actor is supposed to do?" I asked. "No," said Michel. I thought to hell with it, and read the speech again, throwing it all away. At once it came to life…'
90 Adopting the pseudonym Jacques Duchesne, Saint-Denis produced the daily broadcast *Les Français parlent aux Français*.
91 Saint-Denis was joined by two of his disciples, George Devine and Glen Byam Shaw.
92 Hall, *Making an Exhibition of Myself*, p.146.
93 Addenbrooke, *The Royal Shakespeare Company: the Peter Hall Years*, p.197-98.
94 Hall, *Making an Exhibition of Myself*, p.160-61.
95 Michel Saint-Denis, 'A Studio for Experiment and Training', in *Crucial Years*, p.23-4.
96 See *Threads of Time*, p.7.
97 A wartime degree lasted for only five terms. Brook studied French, German and Russian.
98 J.C. Trewin, *Peter Brook: a Biography* (London: Macdonald, 1971), p.20.
99 *Threads of Time*, p.38.
100 Ibid., p.38.
101 Peter Brook, 'What About Real Life?', in *Crucial Years*, p.20-22.
102 *Threads of Time*, p.34.
103 Ibid., p.135.
104 Holm, *Acting My Life*, p.85.
105 See Ibid., p. 86-87.
106 Brook named the project after the term coined by the French surrealist writer Antonin Artaud (1896-1948).
107 Peter Weiss sent the manuscript to Brook.
108 Micheline Steinber, *Flashback: a Pictorial History, 1879-1979: One Hundred Years of Stratford-upon-Avon and the Royal Shakespeare Company* (RSC Publications, 1985), p.79.
109 Trewin, *Peter Brook: a Biography*, p.145.
110 Interestingly, Trevor Nunn cast the production for Brook. See *Threads of Time*, p.149.

[111] Reported in *The Times*, 26, 28, 31 August, 1 September 1964.
[112] Ibid., p.208.
[113] Trevor Nunn, interviewed in *Sir Peter Hall Remembered*, BBC Four, broadcast on 12 September 2017.
[114] Ibid., p.210.
[115] Helen Mirren had just joined the RSC. See the BBC programme *Ruby Wax Meets Helen Mirren* (1996).
[116] As a student of English at Downing College, Nunn was taught by F.R. Leavis.
[117] See Beauman, *The Royal Shakespeare Company: a History of Ten Decades*, p.289.
[118] Ronald Bryden, 'Villains of a Vicious Circus', *The Observer*, 9 October 1966.
[119] Ibid.
[120] Trevor Nunn, 'Afterword', in Addenbrooke, *The Royal Shakespeare Company: the Peter Hall Years*, p.180.
[121] Ibid., p.183.
[122] Peter Hall, *Peter Hall's Diaries* (London: Hamish Hamilton, 1983), p.13.
[123] Ibid., p.469.
[124] Ibid., p.20.
[125] Administrative Director of the NT.
[126] *Peter Hall's Diaries*, p.34.
[127] Ibid., p.38.
[128] Ibid., p.40.
[129] Ibid., p.52.
[130] See Ibid., p.65-67.
[131] *The Times*, 5 December 1972.
[132] See *Threads of Time*, p.152.
[133] See *The Times*, 24 April 1975.
[134] The RSC converted the space into a theatre (designed by John Napier) with seating for two hundred people.
[135] The five-week residency included the complete (or near-complete) Stratford programme, and took place between the Stratford and London seasons.
[136] Trevor Nunn, 'Looking Back, Looking Forward', in Stanley Wells (ed.), *Summerfolk: Essays Celebrating Shakespeare and the Stratford Theatres*, p.131-32.
[137] Ronald Bryden, 'Nunn's *Hamlet*: a Report from the Kitchen', *The Observer*, 7 June 1970.
[138] *Peter Hall's Diaries*, p.115-16.
[139] Michael Billington, *The Guardian*, 10 September 1976.
[140] Ibid., p.314-15.
[141] Ibid., p.302.
[142] Beauman, *The Royal Shakespeare Company: a History of Ten Decades*, p.269.

[143] See 'Michael Billington profiles Terry Hands', *The Guardian*, 4 July 1991. See also John Higgins, 'Hands full for Terry Hands', *The Times*, 19 October 1977.

[144] It was Sir Peter Daubeny who brought Hands together with Pierre Dux.

[145] Ludmila Mikaël joined the RSC in 1975 to play Katharine in Hands's production of *Henry V*.

[146] See Terry Hands, 'Pierre Dux, Vu d'ailleurs', *Hommage à Pierre Dux* (CF website, 2008). See also Claude Baigneres, 'Où est donc passée la Royal Company?', *Le Figaro*, 15 January 2002.

[147] See *Peter Hall's Diaries*, p.287, 290-2, 301, 306-7, 313-4.

[148] See Trevor Nunn, 'From Conference Hall to Theatre', *This Golden Round: the Royal Shakespeare Company at the Swan* (Stratford-upon-Avon: Mulryne and Shewring, 1989), p.1.

[149] See Ibid., p.1-8.

[150] Quoted in John Higgins, 'Phoenix into Swan in the new theatre of audience contact', *The Times*, 17 April 1986.

[151] Terry Hands, 'Towards the Future', *This Golden Round*, p.159.

[152] Bob Crowley, 'Designing for the Swan', *This Golden Round*, p.86.

[153] John Higgins, 'Phoenix into Swan in the new theatre of audience contact', *The Times*, 17 April 1986.

[154] Imogen Stubbs, 'Acting in the Swan', *This Golden Round*, p.109.

[155] Clive Priestley, *The Financial Affairs and Financial Prospects of the Royal Opera House Covent Garden, Ltd and the Royal Shakespeare Company: Report to the Earl Gowrie* (Her Majesty's Stationery Office, 1983).

[156] The RSC commissioned Michael Reardon, architect of the Swan, to design a new Other Place.

[157] Michael Coveney, 'Another time, an Other Place', *The Observer*, 4 August 1991.

[158] Michael Coveney, 'The Love of the Nightingale', *The Financial Times*, 10 November 1988.

[159] Michael Coveney, 'A Monumental Othello', *The Financial Times*, 26 August 1989.

[160] See, for example, 'Chance for a Bold New Start' and 'Wedded to Calamity', *The Sunday Times*, 16 April 1989; and Nunn's letter in reply, *The Sunday Times*, 23 April 1989.

[161] Sir Geoffrey Cass (b. 1932): chief executive of CUP 1972-92; chairman of the RSC 1985-00.

[162] Terry Hands, 'A Fight to the Final Curtain at the RSC', *The Guardian*, 22 April 1989.

[163] Michael Billington, *The Guardian*, 2 June 1983.

[164] See Nicholas de Jongh, 'The Noble Art of Bloodless Revolution', *The Guardian*, 16 July 1990.

[165] Steven Pimlott, David Leveaux and Phyllida Lloyd alongside Katie

Mitchell, who had previously been Noble's assistant director, and Sam Mendes, who had made his Stratford debut the previous year.

[166] Michael Billington, *One Night Stands: A Critic's View of British Theatre from 1971 to 1991* (London: Nick Hern Books, 1993), p.376.

[167] Michael Billington, *The Guardian*, 1 June 1991.

[168] Noble's wife (they married in 1991).

[169] The Collins's Music Hall, established in the 1860s, had been one of the great variety theatres of London. It burnt down in the 1950s.

[170] During the 2000 open day, in the Swan Theatre, Brian Cox called the RST 'the Odeon next door'.

[171] Details: Advantage West Midlands (£304,000); Stratford District Council (£50,000); Warwickshire County Council (£50,000).

[172] Under the title *This England: the Histories* the RSC performed Shakespeare's continuous history plays in sequence and in repertory between March 2000 and May 2001.

[173] See, for example, Michael Billington, *The Guardian*, 9 May 2001.

[174] Chris Foy.

[175] See David Benedict, 'Is the RSC safe in his hands?', *The Observer*, 31 March 2002.

[176] See Brian Logan, 'Steven Pimlott: Melodrama – go on, you know you love it really', *The Independent*, 16 June 2002.

[177] See *The Sunday Times*, 4 November 2001.

[178] See *The Independent on Sunday*, 24 March 2002. Michael Pennington's defence of the RST was published in *The Guardian*, 16 January 2002.

[179] See Adrian Noble, Letter, *The Stage*, 12 July 2001.

[180] Adrian Noble, 'All's well: A tempest? Far from it, says RSC director Adrian Noble', *The Guardian*, 3 October 2001.

[181] 28 March 2002.

[182] See House of Commons, 'Minutes of evidence taken before the Culture, Media and Sport Committee', Tuesday 8 January 2002.

[183] See *The Stage*, 18 April 2002.

[184] David Hunt, director of *The Roman Actor*. Sean Holmes took over.

[185] Peter Hall's son Edward Hall, director of *Edward III*. Disputes over the casting of the title role and the length of the rehearsal time were cited as reasons for his withdrawal. Anthony Clark took over.

[186] Quoted in *The Guardian*, 26 May 2001, p.13.

[187] Rupert Christiansen, 'Noble ambitions? A string of sparkily energetic productions makes director Michael Boyd a strong candidate for the RSC's top job. On the eve of his new production of *The Tempest*, he talks to Rupert Christiansen', *The Daily Telegraph*, 30 April 2002.

[188] The Courtyard Theatre was designed by Ian Ritchie Architects.

[189] Kenneth Tynan, 'The National Theatre: a Speech to the Royal Society of Arts', *A View of the English Stage, 1944-1965* (London: Methuen, 1984), p.360.

[190] 'Sir Peter Hall: Politicians don't grasp the case for the arts', *The Guardian*, 1 November 2011.

[191] The Royal Shakespeare Company, *Annual Review and Accounts 2010/11* (RSC, 2011), p.6.

[192] Hall, *Making an Exhibition of Myself*, p.145-46.

[193] *Peter Hall's Diaries*, p.369.

Index

Aberg, Maria, 203, 209
Ableman, Paul, 87
Adrian, Max, 58, 60
Afore Night Come, 91
   Daniels 1974, 123
   Williams 1962, 63, 101
Agutter, Jenny, 136
Aix-en-Provence Festival, 174
Albee, Edward, 96
Alchemist, The, 152, 154, 184, 187
   Mendes 1991, 173
Aldwych Theatre, London, 58, 62, 71, 74, 87, 88, 91, 94, 96, 114, 130, 214, 215
Alexander, Bill, 13, 126, 143
All's Well That Ends Well, 185, 195
   Barton 1967, 101
   Nunn 1981, 130, 153, 156
Allam, Roger, 146, 158
Allen, Patrick, 58, 118
Almeida, 209
Andrews, Harry, 41
Annis, Francesca, 125, 155, 159
Anouilh, Jean, 71, 98
Antony and Cleopatra, 137, 155
   Brook 1978, 100, 155
   Noble 1982, 152, 184
   Nunn 1972, 98, 128
Arcadia, 185
Arden of Faversham, 136
Arden, John, 87, 110, 118
Armstrong, Alun, 136, 158
Armstrong, Craig, 194
Arnold, Matthew, 11, 21
Art of Success, The, 124, 142, 158
Artaud, Antonin, 87, 215
Arts Council, 56, 72, 75, 95, 114, 115, 117, 145, 174, 179
Arts Theatre Club, 52, 53, 122

As You Like It, 24, 135, 155
   Aberg 2013, 203
   Elliott 1962, 64
   Hands 1980, 98, 135
   Jones 1967, 101
   Noble 1985, 167
   Nunn 1977, 130
Ashcroft, Peggy, 34, 40, 42, 52, 56, 57, 58, 59, 62, 63, 64, 67, 78, 79, 96, 109, 114, 130, 159, 197
Asquith, H.H., 26
Atkins, Eileen, 209
Attenborough, Michael, 170, 173, 178
Atwell, Hayley, 202
Ayrton, Randle, 25, 30
Badel, Alan, 41
Baker, George, 123
Balcony, The
   Hands 1971, 135
Baldwin, Stanley, 26
Bannen, Ian, 57
Barbican, 75, 114, 137, 138, 145, 173, 177, 180, 195, 215
Barker, Howard, 124, 156
Barnes, Peter, 110
Barton, John, 12, 52, 59, 60, 61, 64, 65, 67, 92, 93, 94, 97, 98, 100, 108, 109, 118, 130, 139, 142, 150, 152, 153, 159, 175
Barton. John, 68
Bates, Alan, 153
Bates, Michael, 41
Bayreuth Festival, 26
BBC, 79, 179
Beale, Simon Russell, 142, 146, 183, 208
Bean, Sean, 142, 158
Beatles, The, 66
Beaumont, Binkie, 40, 57, 71, 72

Becket
    Hall 1961, 71, 98, 99
Beckett, Samuel, 86, 171
Beggar's Opera, The, 84, 98
Behean, Katy, 137, 144, 158
Belgrade Theatre, Coventry, 108
Belmondo, Jean-Paul, 84
Bennetts Associates, 198
Benson, Frank, 24, 172
Benthall, Michael, 36, 38, 41, 72
Bernhardt, Sarah, 21
Berry, Cicely, 130
Bingo, 124
Birmingham Rep, 34, 35, 84, 101
Birmingham University, 134
Birthday Party, The, 65, 97
Blakely, Colin, 158
Blakemore, Michael, 115
Blood Wedding, 53
Bloom, Claire, 37
Bogdanov, Michael, 157
Bond, Edward, 124, 125, 137, 155
Bond, Samantha, 185
Bones, Ken, 136
Boswell, Laurence, 195, 201
Bouffes du Nord, Paris, 84
Boyd, Michael, 173, 178, 193, 194, 195, 196, 197, 198, 199, 201, 202, 204, 209, 218
Boyle, Danny, 146
Bradley, David, 136, 183
Branagh, Kenneth, 156, 173, 197
Breaking the Silence, 155
Brecht, Bertolt, 87, 123, 125, 166
Brenton, Howard, 145
Bridges-Adams, William, 24, 27, 28, 29, 35, 52, 212
Brierley, David, 114, 117, 143, 170, 177, 178
Bristol University, 166
Britton, Jasper, 208
Broken Heart, The
    Boyd 1994, 173, 194
Brook, Peter, 12, 35, 38, 42, 52, 56, 61, 62, 64, 65, 66, 68, 75, 78, 79, 80, 83, 84, 85, 86, 87, 88, 89, 91, 92, 96, 97, 100, 101, 109, 110, 114, 121, 122, 125, 135, 151, 152, 155, 159, 185, 186, 212, 215
Brown, Pamela, 30

Bruce, Brenda, 34, 111, 153
Büchner, Georg, 171
Bundle, The, 124
Burgess, Anthony, 136, 145
Burgtheater, Vienna, 135
Burton, Richard, 41, 72, 197
Bury, John, 61, 65, 66, 69, 108, 137, 199
Byam Shaw, Glen, 42, 43, 45, 52, 53, 56, 78, 213, 215
Cabaret, 150
Caird, John, 126, 130, 143, 184
Calder, David, 172, 183
Cambridge Theatre, London, 58
Cambridge University, 52, 92, 108
Camino Real, 53
    Pimlott 1997, 173
Cardenio, 195
Carlisle, John, 136, 158
Caron, Leslie, 52, 53, 67, 95
Cass, Geoffrey, 146, 170, 177, 178, 217
Castle, The, 156
Cats, 134
Censorship, 91, 92
Centre National Dramatique de l'Est, Strasbourg, 79
Changeling, The, 166
Chekhov, Anton, 130, 141, 173
Cherry Orchard, The
    Noble 1995, 142, 184, 185, 186
    Saint-Denis 1961, 57, 63, 79, 97, 99, 150
Children of the Sun, 155
Chitty Chitty Bang Bang, 179
Chitty, Alison, 175
Christie, Julie, 64
Church, Tony, 64, 123, 125
Clockwork Orange, A, 145
Clopton Bridge, Stratford, 23
Clunes, Alec, 52, 53
Cohen, Alexander, 65
Collection, The
    Hall 1962, 65
Collins's Music Hall, 174
Comédie-Française
    (Paris), 11, 12, 13, 21, 22, 135, 180
Comedy of Errors, 186
    Nunn 1976, 125, 130, 150, 152

Williams 1962, 63, 99, 100, 151, 186
Compagnie des Quinze, 78
Congreve, William, 166
Cooke, Dominic, 94, 195, 202
Copeau, Jacques, 61, 78
Coriolanus, 184, 187
    Barton 1967, 100, 101
    Hall 1959, 66
    Hands 1977, 135
Council for the Shakespeare Memorial Association, 23
Country Wife, The, 185
Courtyard Theatre, Stratford, 195, 197, 198, 199, 201
Cox, Brian, 218
Cox, Claire, 185
Cozier, Eric, 35
Cries from Casement, 156
Crowley, Bob, 140, 142, 168
Crucible, The
    Cooke 2006, 202
Culture, Media and Sport Select Committee, 179
Cusack, Niamh, 142, 158
Cusack, Sinéad, 136, 142, 155, 167
Cymbeline, 150, 152, 156, 185
    Gaskill 1963, 99
    Hall 1957, 56, 61, 66
    Noble 1997, 172, 183, 186
Cyrano de Bergerac
    Hands 1983, 136
Dalton, Timothy, 135, 156
Dance of Death, The, 155
Daniels, Ron, 13, 123, 124, 126, 137, 143, 184
Daubeny, Peter, 217
Davies, Howard, 13, 123, 124, 126
Days of the Commune, 154
De la Tour, Frances, 89
De Nobili, Lila, 56
Dear, Nick, 124, 142, 146
Death of a Salesman, 209
Deathwatch, 157
Delicate Balance, A, 96
Demeger, Roger, 142
Dench, Jeffery, 111, 136, 159
Dench, Judi, 58, 63, 94, 111, 125, 143, 150, 152, 178, 179, 197, 202
Denver Center for the Performing Arts, 94
Destiny, 124, 125
Devils, The, 72, 98
    Wood 1961, 72
Devine, George, 42, 44, 78, 215
Doctor Faustus, 83, 157, 210
    Williams 1968, 98
Dodgshun and Unsworth, 23
Dolan, Monica, 185
Doll's House, A
    Noble 1980, 144, 166
Don Quixote, 195
Donmar Warehouse, 87, 91, 124
Donnell, Patrick, 115
Donnellan, Declan, 180
Doran, Gregory, 173, 178, 180, 181, 193, 194, 195, 201, 202, 208
Dotrice, Roy, 58, 64
Double Falsehood, 195
Downie, Penny, 142, 158, 202
Drama Centre, London, 166
Duchêne, Kate, 185
Duchess of Malfi, 96, 98, 150, 156, 166
Dumb Waiter, The, 122
Duras, Marguerite, 96
Dutch Uncle, 96
Dux, Pierre, 136, 217
Easter
    Mitchell 1995, 173
Eastward Ho!, 181
Edgar, David, 111, 124, 125, 145, 153, 175
Edinburgh Festival, 108
Edinburgh University, 194
Edward III, 181
Edward, Prince of Wales, 28
Egeraat, Erick van, 174
Electra, 79
Elgar, Edward, 28
Elgar's Rondo, 186
Eliot, T.S., 85, 101, 134, 173
Elliott, Denholm, 59
Empty Space, The (Brook), 38
Engel, Susan, 64
English Stage Company, 44
Epicene, 123
Erdman, Nikolai, 152
Escoffier, Auguste, 33

Evans, Edith, 34, 78
Every Good Boy Deserves Favour, 154
Every Man in His Humour, 184
Everyone's Shakespeare, 173
Fair Maid of the West, 143
Falstaff
   (Elgar), 28
Family Reunion, 85
Farmer, George, 115, 116, 119
Farr, David, 203, 209
Farrah, 62
Farran, Lynda, 170
Faust, 157
Fearon, Ray, 185, 203
Fernald, John, 53
Ffrangcon-Davies, Gwen, 34
Fielding, Emma, 185, 194
Fielding, Susannah, 203
Fiennes, Ralph, 146, 157, 168, 197
Finney, Albert, 72
Flannery, Peter, 124, 146, 156, 184
Fleetwood, Susan, 94, 118, 146, 153
Fletcher, John, 181, 195, 208
Flower, Archibald, 24, 25, 27, 33
Flower, Charles, 19, 24
Flower, Dennis, 170
Flower, Edgar, 24
Flower, Fordham, 33, 37, 40, 45, 56, 92, 95, 212
Fool, The, 124, 155
Ford Davies, Oliver, 202, 208
Ford, John, 141, 185, 194
Forest, The, 144, 166
Four Seasons, 134
Foy, Chris, 218
Fremantle, John
   (Lord Cottesloe), 72, 74
Freshwater, Geoffrey, 158
Gaiety Theatre
   (London), 21
Gale, Mariah, 203
Gambon, Michael, 136, 152, 158, 159, 178, 184
García Lorca, 53
Gaskill, William, 57, 99
Gems, Pam, 124
Genet, Jean, 87, 91, 157
Ghosts
   Mitchell 1993, 173
Gibson, Patrick, 115
Gide, Andre, 53
Gielgud, John, 40, 42, 43, 56, 57, 63, 78, 79, 96, 97, 213
Gilbreath, Alexandra, 185, 194, 203, 209
Giraudoux, Jean, 71
Glasgow Citizens', 156
Glen, Iain, 185, 194, 202
Glenister, Robert, 172, 185
Glover, Julian, 208
Godfrey, Derek, 58, 98, 136
Goethe, Johann Wolfgang, 171
Goldoni, Carlo, 171, 184
Good, 124
Goodbody, Buzz, 123, 124, 151, 152, 160
Goodman, Arnold, 73, 114, 115, 116
Goodman, Henry, 142, 209
Goodwin, John, 116
Goold, Rupert, 203, 209
Gorky, Maxim, 151, 152, 155, 159, 186
Government Inspector, The
   Hall 1966, 102
Granville-Barker, Harley, 11, 13, 24, 26, 150, 212
Gray, Simon, 96
Greeks, The, 94, 152
Green, Dorothy, 35
Green, Julien, 53
Greene, Graham, 85
Gresham School, 83
Griffiths, Richard, 94, 158
Guinness, Alec, 78
Guthrie, Tyrone, 29
Gwilym, Mike, 123, 125, 130, 143, 152
Haig, David, 142
Hall, Peter, 11, 19, 29, 35, 42, 45, 52, 53, 56, 57, 58, 59, 60, 61, 62, 64, 65, 66, 75, 78, 79, 80, 81, 83, 85, 89, 91, 92, 94, 95, 96, 97, 98, 99, 101, 102, 108, 109, 114, 115, 116, 117, 118, 119, 122, 125, 128, 136, 137, 139, 151, 157, 159, 175, 180, 185, 187, 197, 198, 199, 213, 214, 215, 216, 217, 218, 219
Halliday, Peter, 41
Hamlet, 24, 52, 85, 87, 93, 122, 123, 152, 184, 185, 195

Barton 1980, 93, 98, 153
Benthall 1948, 37, 101
Daniels 1989, 145
Farr 2013, 203
Goodbody 1975, 123, 151
Hall 1965, 64, 66, 68, 97, 99, 100, 153, 159
Hall 1966, 101
Noble 1992, 156, 171, 183, 186, 187
Nunn 1970, 128, 151, 152, 153, 159
Pimlott 2000, 173
Hampton, Christopher, 124, 155
Hands Off Our Theatre (HOOT), 178
Hands, Marina, 135
Hands, Terry, 12, 62, 97, 98, 101, 109, 122, 134, 135, 136, 137, 139, 141, 142, 143, 145, 146, 150, 151, 153, 155, 160, 170, 173, 178, 197, 199, 217
Hansel and Gretel, 124
Hardy, Thomas, 26
Hare, David, 119
Harris, Amanda, 141, 142, 146, 184, 202
Harris, Robert, 35
Harrison, Howard, 172
Harrow, Lisa, 94, 111
Hassell, Alex, 203, 208
Helpmann, Robert, 37
Henry IV, 25, 28, 41, 52, 101, 156, 184, 208
Boyd 2007, 197
Hands 1975, 97, 135, 153
Noble 1991, 171, 182, 186
Nunn 1982, 138, 153, 156
Quayle/Redgrave 1951, 41
Henry V, 41, 185, 186, 208, 217
Boyd 2007, 197
Hands 1975, 135
Noble 1984, 156, 159, 167
Quayle 1951, 41
Henry VI, 167, 194
Boyd 2000, 174
Boyd 2007, 197
Hands 1977, 135, 152, 153, 155
Henry VIII, 185, 186, 187
Doran 1996, 173

Nunn 1969, 111
Henry, Guy, 185
Heywood, Thomas, 143, 184
Heywood, Vikki, 195
Hicks, Greg, 202
Hinds, Ciarán, 146
Hippolytus, 124
Histories, The
Hall/Barton 1964, 64, 98, 99
Hitchcock, Alfred, 186
Hobson, Harold, 59, 60, 69, 71
Hogg, Ian, 186
Holm, Ian, 40, 43, 58, 59, 63, 64, 66, 68, 97, 101, 146, 197, 203
Holman, Robert, 124
Holy Trinity Church, Stratford, 23
Homecoming, The, 65, 203
Hall 1965, 64, 98, 101
Hoskins, Bob, 166
Hotel Astoria, 45, 56
Hove, Ivo van, 209
Howard, Alan, 89, 100, 101, 108, 135, 151, 155, 159, 197
Hughes, Ian, 185
Hutchinson, Ron, 124
Hyde, Jonathan, 136, 203
Hynes, Garry, 144
Hytner, Nicholas, 146, 184
Ian Ritchie Architects, 218
Ibsen, Henrik, 141, 150, 154, 166, 171, 173
Investigation, The
Brook 1965, 100, 153
Ionesco, Eugene, 53
Irons, Jeremy, 142, 157
Irving, Henry, 20
Island of the Mighty, The, 118
Island Princess, The, 181
Jackson, Barry, 27, 33, 34, 38, 40, 42, 52, 84, 101, 212
Jackson, Glenda, 64, 87, 88, 100, 101, 150
Jacobi, Derek, 136, 155
James, Emrys, 94, 111, 118, 153
Jefford, Barbara, 42, 160
Jeffrey, Peter, 64
Jennings, Alex, 146, 184
Jesson, Paul, 185
Johnson, Richard, 98
Joint Council of the National Theatre,

72
Jones, David, 12, 62, 109, 118
Jones, Gemma, 89, 158
Jones, Griffith, 123, 125, 159
Jonson, Ben, 123, 141
Julius Caesar, 157, 184, 185, 186
   Nunn 1972, 98
Juno and the Paycock, 130, 150, 156
Kane, John, 89, 108, 186
Kempson, Rachel, 29
Kestelman, Sara, 89, 136, 158
Killick, David, 158
King John, 84, 92
   Aberg 2012, 203
   Barton 1974, 92
   Warner 1988, 143
King Lear, 86, 137, 151, 152, 157, 184, 186, 208
   Brook 1962, 64, 66, 86, 97, 99, 101, 151, 185
   Donnellan 2002, 180
   Farr 2010, 203
   Gielgud 1950, 42
   Goodbody 1964, 123
   Hytner 1990, 146
   Komisarjevsky 1937, 30
   Noble 1982, 156, 166
   Noble 1993, 171, 183
   Nunn 1976, 125, 129, 150, 151, 153
   Nunn 2007, 203
Kingsley, Ben, 89, 123, 143, 151
Kitchen, Michael, 142, 158
Kleist, Heinrich von, 171
Koch, Frederick, 139
Kohler, Estelle, 100, 101, 118, 135, 159
Koltai, Ralph, 62
Koltès, Bernard-Marie, 171
Komisarjevsky, Theodore, 27, 29, 30, 36
Kott, Jan, 86
Krige, Alice, 136
Kustow, Michael, 122
Kyle, Barry, 13, 126, 137, 141, 143
Lady from the Sea, 84
Lambert, Mikel, 123
LAMDA, 87, 88, 91
Lapotaire, Jane, 94, 187
Lark, The, 98
Last Days of Don Juan, 146
Laughton, Charles, 52
Laurie, John, 25
Lawrence of Arabia, 72
Leigh-Hunt, Barbara, 125
Leighton, Margaret, 34
Leningrad, 56
Lennon, Peter, 144
Lesser, Anton, 155, 168, 197
Levin, Bernard, 68
Lewis, Damian, 185
Liaisons dangereuses, Les, 124, 144, 155
Light, John, 185
Little Eyolf, 185
   Noble 1996, 142, 183
Littler, Emile, 57, 91
Littler, Prince, 57, 58, 72
Littlewood, Joan, 61
Liverpool Everyman, 134
Lloyd Webber, Andrew, 134
Lloyd, Selwyn, 73
Lockyer, Mark, 209
London Assurance, 155
London Theatre Studio, 78
Look Back in Anger, 134
Lord Alexander, 177
Lord Chamberlain, 91
Lord of the Flies, 84
Losey, Joseph, 186
Loud Boy's Life, The, 124
Love for Love, 166
Love of the Nightingale, The, 143
Love's Labour's Lost, 29, 52, 84, 93, 94, 100, 152, 153, 159, 187
   Barton 1965, 100
   Barton 1978, 93, 153
   Brook 1946, 35, 52, 84, 101
   Hall 1956, 56
   Hands 1990, 146, 157, 183, 184
Lower Depths, The
   Robertson 1962, 63
Lunghi, Cherie, 158
Lynch, Finbar, 184
Lyttelton, Oliver (Lord Chandos), 72, 73, 74
Macbeth, 29, 78, 98, 125, 156, 184, 186
   Byam Shaw 1955, 43
   Doran 1999, 173

Gielgud 1952, 42
Hall 1967, 102
Noble 1986, 142, 143, 155, 157, 167
Nunn 1974, 152
Nunn 1976, 124, 128, 129, 144, 150, 152, 154, 160
MacDonald, Ramsay, 26
Mackintosh, Cameron, 138, 196
Madeley, Anna, 185
Magdalen College, Oxford, 83
Magee, Patrick, 64, 65, 88
Magic Flute, The, 95
Maid's Tragedy, The, 155
Maids, The, 157
Malaya Bronnaya Theatre, Moscow, 194
Malcontent, The, 94, 181
Man and Superman, 84
Man is Man, 123, 166
Man of Mode, The, 152
    Hands 1971, 135
Manchester Royal Exchange, 166
Mannion, Tom, 136
Manville, Lesley, 158
Marat/Sade, 87, 88, 91
    Brook 1964, 64, 87, 100, 151, 186
Marivaux, 171
Marlowe, Christopher, 83, 141
Marowitz, Charles, 87
Marston, John, 94
Mason, Brewster, 64, 65, 97, 111, 197
Masson, Forbes, 203
Master Builder, The
    Noble 1989, 145, 168
McCabe, Richard, 146, 183, 203
McCowen, Alec, 64, 183, 185
McDiarmid, Ian, 125
McDonagh, Martin, 175
McGuckin, Aislín, 203
McIntosh, Genista, 170
McKellen, Ian, 124, 125, 144, 154, 203
McTeer, Janet, 142
Measure for Measure, 85, 150, 153, 155, 184, 185
    Barton 1970, 100, 101
    Boyd 1998, 194
    Brook 1950, 42, 85
    Noble 1983, 155, 160, 167

Meiningen Company, 22
Melia, Joe, 142
Mendes, Sam, 141, 146, 160, 173
Mercer, David, 110
Merchant of Venice, The, 29, 150, 156
    Benthall 1947, 36
    Goold 2011, 203
    Langham 1960, 59
Merchant, Vivien, 64
Mermaid Theatre, London, 143
Merry Wives of Windsor, 151, 153, 186, 195
    Hands 1968, 100, 134
    Hands 1975, 97
    Nunn 1979, 130
Middleton and Rowley, 166
Midsummer Night's Dream, 28, 89, 96, 122, 155, 184, 195
    Boyd 1999, 174, 194
    Brook 1970, 89, 129, 151, 159
    Hall 1959, 66
    Hall 1962, 99
    Noble 1994, 172, 184
Mikaël, Ludmila, 135, 217
Millson, Joseph, 209
Mirren, Helen, 97, 135, 136, 143, 151, 152, 159, 166, 184
Misérables, Les, 138
Mitchell, Katie, 173
Moderato Cantabile, 84
Moiseiwitsch, Tanya, 41
Molière, 11, 21, 171
Moreau, Jeanne, 84
Morley, Christopher, 108, 111
Moscow Gold, 145
Mother Courage, 150
Much Ado About Nothing, 24, 93, 94, 136, 152, 184, 186
    Barton 1976, 93, 125, 150
    Boyd 1996, 194
    Gielgud 1950, 42
Murder in the Cathedral, 134, 135, 186
    Pimlott 1993, 173
Murphy, Gerard, 140, 142, 156, 157
Napier, John, 216
National Theatre, 24, 26, 44, 62, 72, 74, 75, 79, 94, 114, 115, 116, 117, 118, 119, 124, 136, 170, 182, 198,

216, 218
Nettles, John, 125
Newcastle residency, 124
Nicholas Nickleby
   Nunn/Caird 1980, 130, 152
Nichols, Peter, 110
Nicholson, Yvonne, 123
Nixon, Pippa, 203
Noah, 78
Noble, Adrian, 13, 101, 125, 126,
   137, 141, 143, 146, 152, 155, 156,
   157, 159, 160, 166, 167, 170, 171,
   172, 173, 174, 175, 177, 178, 179,
   180, 182, 186, 193, 195, 196, 197,
   199, 217, 218
Normington, John, 64
Northam, Jeremy, 185
Novello Theatre, London, 196
Nunn, Trevor, 12, 62, 65, 95, 98,
   101, 108, 109, 111, 114, 115, 116,
   117, 118, 119, 121, 122, 123, 124,
   125, 126, 128, 130, 134, 136, 137,
   138, 139, 141, 142, 143, 145, 150,
   151, 152, 154, 156, 157, 159, 160,
   171, 185, 186, 187, 199, 203, 209,
   215, 216, 217
O'Brien, Timothy, 134
O'Neill, Jonjo, 203
O'Toole, Peter, 58, 59, 60, 71, 72, 75,
   92, 96
Odéon, Paris, 136, 180
Odyssey, The, 184
Oedipus Rex, 79
Old Times, 96
Old Vic, 29, 41, 42, 62, 73, 78, 79,
   96, 166
Olivier, Laurence, 34, 40, 43, 52, 56,
   62, 63, 66, 67, 73, 74, 75, 78, 79,
   84, 85, 96, 115, 116, 117, 151,
   156
Ondine, 71
Oresteia, The, 94
Osborne, John, 134
Otello, 136
Othello, 153, 185, 186
   Attenborough 1999, 173
   Nunn 1989, 154, 157
   Zeffirelli 1961, 57
Other Place, Stratford, 81, 123, 124,
   128, 130, 143, 166, 171, 175, 180,

196, 197
Oxford Playhouse, 53
Pallot, Nicky, 170
Paoli, Cécile, 158
Paris, 21, 53, 64, 68, 71, 78, 96, 135,
   180, 210
Parker, Nathaniel, 142
Pasco, Richard, 93, 94, 111, 158
Payne, Ben Iden, 30
Pearce, Joanne, 157, 168, 172, 183
Peck, Bob, 123, 125, 136, 143, 158
Peer Gynt, 137, 184, 185
   Barton 1994, 142, 175
Pennington, Michael, 94, 125, 153,
   178, 218
Penny for a Song, A, 150
Pericles, 135
   Daniels 1979, 124
   Hands 1969, 100, 111, 153
Perse School, Cambridge, 52
Peter Grimes
   (Britten), 35
Phillips, Siân, 58
Phoenix Theatre, London, 78, 85
Physicists, The
   Brook 1963, 99
Piaf, 124
Pigott-Smith, Tim, 202
Pillars of the Community, 150, 154
Pimlott, Steven, 173, 178, 218
Pinter, Harold, 62, 63, 64, 96, 97, 98,
   110, 159, 203
Piper, Tom, 195
Pirandello, Luigi, 52
Pit Theatre, London, 137
Place, The, 122
Plantagenets, The
   Noble 1988, 145, 155, 157, 159,
   167, 183
Playing Shakespeare, 94
Plummer, Christopher, 72
Poliakoff, Stephen, 124, 155
Porter, Eric, 58, 64, 71, 98, 151, 159
Postlethwaite, Pete, 136, 142, 158
Powell, Michael, 152
Power and the Glory, 85
Priestley Report, 217
Priestley, Clive, 170
Pringle, Bryan, 65
Profumo, John, 74

Project Fleet, 177, 178
Proposal, The, 122
Pryce, Jonathan, 142, 155, 156, 157, 167
Quarshie, Hugh, 140, 142, 156, 157
Quayle, Anthony, 37, 40, 41, 42, 44, 53, 56, 197, 213
Queen's Theatre, London, 43, 78
RADA, 134
Reardon, Michael, 139, 217
Recruiting Officer, 166
Redgrave, Michael, 40, 41, 78, 99, 197, 215
Redgrave, Vanessa, 64, 99, 150
Rees, Roger, 111, 125, 143, 152
Reeves, Saskia, 185
Relapse, The, 109
Renaissance Theatre Company, 156
Retour d'Ulysse dans sa patrie, Le, 174
Revenger's Tragedy, 108, 156
   Nunn 1966, 100, 108, 151
Revolutions Season, 202
Reza, Yasmina, 171
Richard II, 29, 41, 93, 94, 97, 157, 184, 208
   Barton 1971, 100
   Barton 1973, 93
   Boyd 2007, 197
   Daniels 1990, 146
   Hands 1980, 135
   Pimlott 2000, 173
   Quayle 1951, 41
Richard III, 100, 122, 134, 135, 155, 167, 184, 194
   Boyd 2007, 197
   Hands 1970, 100, 152, 153
   Hands 1980, 98, 135, 155
   Mendes 1992, 173
Richardson, Ian, 58, 88, 93, 94, 100, 146
Richardson, Joely, 142
Richardson, Ralph, 34
Rickman, Alan, 158
Ridings, Richard, 146
Rigby, Terence, 64
Rigg, Diana, 58, 64
Roache, Linus, 146, 158
Roaring Girl, The, 152
Robbe-Grillet, Alain, 87
Robeson, Paul, 96
Rockefeller, John D., 26
Rodway, Norman, 108, 146, 157
Rogers, Paul, 64
Roman Actor, The, 181
Romans, The, 118, 128, 186
Romeo and Juliet, 29, 152, 153, 157, 186, 194
   Attenborough 1997, 173
   Bogdanov 1986, 142
   Boyd 2000, 194
   Brook 1947, 36, 101
   Byam Shaw 1958, 98
   Goold 2010, 203
   Hands 1973, 135
   Koun 1967, 101
   Noble 1995, 172
   Nunn 1976, 125, 130, 153
Root, Amanda, 146, 158
Rose, Clifford, 64, 186
Rosencrantz and Guildenstern are Dead, 66
Roundhouse, 122, 180, 197
Rover, The, 142, 157, 184, 208
Royal Court, London, 44, 151, 156
Royal Hunt of the Sun, 182
Royal Opera House, London, 85, 95, 170, 217
Royal Shakespeare Theatre, 19, 130, 166, 174, 177, 178, 195, 196, 197, 198, 199, 214, 218
RSC Academy, 180, 196
Rudkin, David, 91, 110, 124, 153, 155, 156
Ruf, Éric, 180
Russell, Ken, 152
Rutherford, Mary, 158
Rylance, Mark, 136, 146, 158
Rylands, George, 52
Saint Catharine's College, Cambridge, 213
Saint-Denis, Michel, 12, 57, 61, 62, 65, 78, 79, 80, 81, 84, 89, 96, 97, 121, 122, 125, 150, 186, 215
Savoy Hotel, London, 33
Schiller, Friedrich, 171
School for Scandal, 185
Scofield, Paul, 35, 36, 37, 57, 58, 64, 84, 85, 86, 101, 159
Scorsese, Martin, 186
Scott, Elizabeth, 26, 27

Screens, The, 87, 91
　Brook 1964, 87
Seagull, The
　Hands 1990, 141, 146, 183
　Noble 2000, 185, 186
　Nunn 2007, 203
Sentimental Journey, 83
Shakespeare Complete Works Festival, 196
Shakespeare Memorial Theatre, 52, 139
Shakespeare, William, 26, 28, 41, 57, 62, 66, 80, 85, 86, 89, 92, 94, 109, 122, 124, 139, 141, 166, 175, 181, 195, 196, 202, 213, 218
Shaw, Bernard, 11, 13, 24, 25, 26, 34
Shaw, Sebastian, 25, 159
Shelton, Thomas, 195
Sheppard, Morgan, 88
Sher, Antony, 136, 156, 202, 208
Silence, 124
Silver Tassie, The, 152
Simon, Josette, 136
Sinden, Donald, 35, 64, 94, 97, 111, 125, 150, 151, 153, 178, 197
Singer, 146, 156, 184
Slinger, Jonathan, 203
Small-scale Tour, 124
Smith, Maggie, 150
Somerset Maugham, 53
Sons of Light, The, 124, 155
Sophocles, 94, 171
Spanish Tragedy, The, 194
　Boyd 1997, 174
Spiegel, Sam, 72
Spriggs, Elizabeth, 64
Stanton, Barry, 89, 186
Staunton, Imelda, 142
Stephens, Katy, 203
Stephens, Robert, 172, 182
Stephens, Toby, 184, 202
Stevenson, Juliet, 155, 156
Stewart, Patrick, 89, 125, 143, 151, 202
Stoppard, Tom, 66, 110, 154, 184, 185
Storry, Malcolm, 158, 202
Strange Case of Dr Jekyll and Mr Hyde, The, 145
Strauss, Botho, 171

Strindberg, August, 152, 155, 185
Stubbs, Imogen, 140, 142, 144, 146, 157
Studio, Stratford, 79
Suchet, David, 123, 143, 154
Suicide, The, 152
Sullivan, Barry, 23
Summerfolk, 152
Sunday Times, 145, 217, 218
Suzman, Janet, 64, 65, 100, 109, 151
Swan Theatre, Stratford, 138, 139, 140, 141, 143, 173, 174, 180, 194, 196, 197, 198, 201, 208, 217, 218
Taaffe, Emily, 203
Tamburlaine the Great
　Hands 1992, 173
Tamer Tamed, The, 195
Taming of the Shrew, 92, 109, 155, 184, 185, 195
　Barton 1960, 92, 96
　Nunn 1967, 100, 109
Tango, 108
Tantalus, 94, 175
Taylor, C.P., 124
Taylor, Valerie, 35
Teale, Owen, 185
Teatro Stabile di Genova, 135
Tempest, The, 25, 151, 184, 186, 208, 218
　Barton 1970, 101
　Benthall 1951, 41
　Farr 2012, 203
　Mendes 1993, 173
　Noble 1998, 172, 183, 186
Tennant, David, 185, 194, 195, 202, 208
Theatre Act (1843), 91
Théâtre du Vieux Colombier, Paris, 78
Theatre of Cruelty, 87, 88, 91, 121
　Brook 1964, 64, 87, 100
Théâtre Sarah-Bernhardt, Paris, 64
Theatre Workshop, 61
Theatregoround, 62, 122, 134
Thebans, The, 157, 171, 183, 186, 187
Theobald, Lewis, 195
Thomas, Charles, 64, 111
Three Sisters, 79, 152, 154, 160, 215
　Nunn 1978, 125

Nunn 1979, 130
Threlfall, David, 158
Thwarting of Baron Bolligrew, 108
Timon of Athens, 166
   Schlesinger 1965, 100, 102
Titus Andronicus, 85, 166
   Brook 1955, 43, 61, 64, 66, 85
   Nunn 1972, 101
   Warner 1987, 141
Travesties
   Noble 1993, 184
Trewin, J.C., 215
Troilus and Cressida, 135, 153, 160, 184, 186, 187
   Hall 1960, 58, 60, 66, 98, 99
   Hands 1981, 135
   Mendes 1990, 141, 146, 183, 184
Troughton, David, 136, 142, 184, 209
Troughton, Sam, 203
Turner, Graham, 158, 209
Tutin, Dorothy, 58, 63, 98
Twelfth Night, 93, 94, 97, 135, 152, 153, 154, 185, 186, 187, 202
   Barton 1969, 93, 97, 101, 111, 150
   Farr 2012, 203
   Gielgud 1955, 43
   Hall 1958, 56
   Hall 1960, 59, 98, 99
   Hands 1979, 135, 136
   Noble 1997, 172
   Williams 1966, 98, 99, 101
Twin Rivals, The, 153
Two Gentlemen of Verona, 59
   Phillips 1970, 101, 152
Two Noble Kinsmen, The, 208
   Kyle 1986, 140, 157, 184
Tynan, Kenneth, 36, 42, 63, 75, 198, 212, 213, 214, 218
Ubu Rex, 166
Uncle Vanya, 123, 187
   Mitchell 1998, 173
Under Milk Wood, 122
Ure, Mary, 66
Urquhart, Philippa, 87
US, 88, 92
   Brook 1966, 88, 100, 151, 186
Verga, Giovanni, 171
Victor, 91

View from the Bridge, 166, 209
Villard, Jean, 78
Vitrac, Roger, 91
Voss, Philip, 187
Wagner, Richard, 26
Waites, Zoë, 185
Waiting for Godot, 53
Walcott, Derek, 184
Waldmann, Alex, 203
Waller, David, 64, 89, 125, 136, 159
Walter, Harriet, 130, 156, 202
Wanamaker, Zoë, 158
Warner, David, 64, 66, 68, 75, 99, 100, 146, 153, 159, 202
Warner, Deborah, 141, 143, 146
Wars of the Roses, 93
   Hall 1963, 66, 68, 97, 98, 99, 100, 159
Watteau, Antoine, 84
Webster, John, 141
Wedekind, Frank, 171
Weiss, Peter, 87, 91, 100, 153, 215
Wells, Stanley, 170
Wertenbaker, Timberlake, 143
Wesker, Arnold, 134
West End, 40, 52, 57, 85, 91, 137, 179, 196
Westminster School, London, 83
Whelan, Peter, 124, 175, 183
When Thou Art King, 159
White, Willard, 144
Whiting, John, 68, 72, 98, 110
Whybrow, Lucy, 185
Wilkinson, Norman, 28
Wilkinson, Tom, 158
Willatt, Hugh, 114
Williams, Clifford, 12, 61, 63, 65, 87, 151, 186
Williams, Michael, 64, 89, 109, 125, 150
Williams, Olivia, 185, 194
Williams, Tennessee, 53
Williamson, Nicol, 123, 152
Wilson, Stuart, 123
Wilton, Penelope, 202
Winter's Tale, 96, 98, 101, 152, 156, 185
   Doran 1998, 173
   Noble 1992, 171, 183
   Nunn 1969, 111, 128, 150, 153

Witch of Edmonton, The, 78, 155, 156
Wolfit, Donald, 30
Woman Killed With Kindness, A, 184, 185
   Mitchell 1991, 173
Women Beware Women, 135
   Boswell 2006, 202
   Hands 1969, 111, 150
   Page 1962, 63

Wood, Clive, 136
Wood, John, 146, 154, 168, 184
Wood, Peter, 52
Woodeson, Nicholas, 142, 144
Woodvine, John, 125, 158
Wright, Nicholas, 124
Wynyard, Diana, 37
Young Vic, 180, 209
Zeffirelli, Franco, 57

www.ingramcontent.com/pod-product-compliance
Lightning Source LLC
Chambersburg PA
CBHW030257100526
44590CB00012B/433